Once upon a Tree

Calvin Miller

BAKER BOOK HOUSE
Grand Rapids, Michigan 49516

Contents

Preface   7

Introduction   11

The Nail That Holds All

The Cross and the Issue of Meaning

15

The Wood of the New Agreement

The Cross and the Issue of Salvation

29

The Timbers of Grief

The Cross Answers Our Grieving

45

The Community of the Cross

God's Kingdom and Community

65

The Tree of Treachery

When We Are Traitors—When We Are Betrayed

85

Who Caused the Cross?

Answering Our Own Accountability

105

The Death of Death

Afraid of Neither Death nor Dying

119

The Dying Life

The Art of Sacrificing Ourselves

137

The Piercing of Pain

The Triumph of the Cross in Our Suffering

157

The Triumph of Transcendence

Living Here, Living Somewhere Else, But Ever Living

175

Notes   193

Preface

All I am and hope for is forever riveted to that mysterious moment that freezes history in focus: the cross of Christ! At that pivot of time where nothing moves, I find both excellence and shame. There Jesus' sacrificial death stands embarrassingly close to my self-centeredness. There I bring my greed and beg his generosity. There I bring my trivial whimperings and marvel again how far his suffering is willing to go.

I've asked myself what it is that should so everlastingly bind his dying to my wholeness. I am left dumbfounded at God's saving proposition. Why should my freedom forge the very pinions that hold him to the wood? But gazing upward, I realize that I am stalked by a passionate and illogical love altogether incapable of quitting its pursuit.

Did he really die two thousand years ago? It seems not so. He is dying now—ever dying. I see his cross daily and I am rebuked by my own pursuit of an easy kingdom. I cannot place Good Friday in the distant past. I live too much in its continuing glory; I reckon with its daily demands.

Most of the time, Jesus and I are alone at Calvary—just the two of us. The centurion, the Pharisees, the thieves, the bystanders—all disappear and leave us uncomfortably alone. We are host to each other in a dialogue of Spirit that makes all life possible. At such moments I do not philosophize, I only marvel. In beholding him as he is, I cringe at what I am. But he assures me that even as I am, I remain valuable to God. "Behold my hands," he says, "and you will know how great is your value unto my Father." Here is Emmaus love; and I confess that my heart burns within me even as we talk (see Luke 24:32).

"Come, Jesus," I say, "let me see you etched in dying on my conscience of convenience. Your cross is not a separate event in time. It is now . . . now . . . while I minister to a new widow who sits in the trauma of her grief and bids me give her one good reason for going on with her own life. It presides quietly over an embittered couple whose bitterness must be crucified, if their marriage is to walk out of the tomb where it has all but sealed itself."

All of life is packaged in suffering, and it is severe. His dying is my treasure, for it shows me the "how and why" of my own dying and of my living, too. I am crucified with Christ (Gal. 2:20). I can live wisely only when I remember that each day of my life I must be able to see the hurried approach of my own death. My days are swifter than a weaver's shuttle (Job 7:6). How honest is the psalmist: "[Lord,] Teach us to number our days aright, that we may gain a heart of wisdom" (Ps. 90:12 NIV). The days are precious, for they are few. This Calvary reckoning, therefore, must come not only on Good Fridays, but on Tuesdays as well; indeed the cross is every day's business. So there are ever two crosses: his and mine. At the rare moments of confronting the shortness of our lives, I know a "crossly" brotherhood with Jesus; I glory in the fellowship of his sufferings (Phil. 3:10). For only when we have died together, may we live together. My longings then at last may sleep in his security.

The dying Savior has taught me that his dying alone saves. This is my one great confidence.

Father, into thy hands I commend my spirit. God is the manager of my mortality, and I may live the dying life knowing that all our important affairs are in good hands.

Introduction

used to wonder why the crucifixion week takes up so much space in the four Gospels (it consumes nearly half of John and from a third to a fourth of each of the other Gospels), while the earlier thirty-two years and fifty-one weeks of Jesus' life are crowded into the smaller opening chapters of each. Other writers and thinkers have observed that facing death wonderfully clears the mind and allows us brilliant illumination and focus on the things we really believe. So at the cross the doctrines and philosophies of a thirty-three-year-old field rabbi are pulled into sharp focus. He had taught us not to be afraid, and so at his dying time we are eager to watch him to see if our teacher lives by his teaching. He taught us we would live forever, and here we watch him closely to look for chinks in his confidence. Does it hold? Is he steady and secure before the jeering mob? He taught us to hold to faith and, looking at his cross, we ask, "Did *he*?" He taught us that we should be happy in persecution (Matt. 5:10). Now, at his naked trial, we watch to see if he can live out his own demanding Beatitude.

The cross is his dying place. But Jesus alone is not on trial. All his thought and philosophy must also reply before Pilate. Will it stand? Can it answer? Will he whimper and complain and recant? Will he excoriate his accusers or bless them? Will he turn the other cheek or turn on them in wrath? Will he knock the jeering world to pieces or love it in its bloody cruelty? Here at Calvary the great God passes under the microscope of our scrutiny. The cross tells all and lets us decide if his way really is the truth and the life (John 14:6).

It has been twenty-five years since I first wrote this book. During those years, I have moved an obvious two and a half decades closer to my own death. How do I feel about *his* death as I draw ever closer to *my* own? The cross remains for me the passionate triumph of Christ. I see the same things I saw when I was thirty, but I see them clearer now. His death and dying is still the best teacher on how to do it when my time shall come. But the how-tos of dying are not the only lessons of his cross. There are other critical lessons of Calvary: how to deal with grief, pain, and even meaninglessness.

At the cross I am taught how to deal with grief. I will need that skill well-honed when the time comes! I am taught the essential hope inherent in the riddle of pain. I will really need coaching in this area, for pain terrifies me even as an idea. I am coached by my gracious Lord as to how I must one day look the Medusa of meaninglessness in the face, and not let her serpentine coils freeze me into dull stone.

His cross is not just an answer for my dying. I have also needed the cross in living through these forty-five years of my discipleship. But now, as ever closer, comes life's great finality. I am ready for the cross' best lessons. For soon shall come life's last betrayal, and after that the shame of death, for (let us be reminded once again) we are generally more ashamed of death than afraid of it. This heightened focus that death affords first visited me only a few years ago.

My doctor told me I must go to a specialist, and the specialist told me that I would likely have to have a valve replacement in my heart. I wasn't altogether sure I would die in the near future, but for the first time in my life the possibility loomed before me. Friends who knew the prognosis and my fears prayed for me. Perhaps their prayers were efficacious and perhaps the early prognosis had been hasty, but the glorious end of my story was a joyous reprieve. The operation was unnecessary.

Still, the uncertainty of those days has left my vision clearer about all those things I said that I believed. Death was not as terrifying as I had thought it would be. I escaped the pain yet it seemed somehow bearable ahead of time. I could see myself, like Christ, praying from my little vista of dim finality, "Father, into thy hands."

Now I know the cross *does* answer all! Thus in this book I take in hand a look at those fearsome doctrines of our lives. There are ten of them: human meaning, salvation, grief, the need for community, betrayal, accountability, death and dying, self-sacrifice, pain, and transcendence.

One by one, I shall (for my sake and perhaps for yours) open these dark packages at the cross and expose them to the light of his own gallant dying. I know that when all that "light of sacred story" falls on our fears, we will say with Paul, "Truly the sufferings of this present time are not worthy to be compared with the glory that shall be" (Rom. 8:18).

Come with me to the end of Jesus' life on earth, for only at the end are we able to mark the beginning of any real understanding of the greatest questions of our lives.

13

*B*ut when the fulness
of the time was come,
God sent forth his Son . . .
to redeem them
that were under the law. . . .

Paul of Tarsus
Galatians 4:4–5 KJV

1

The Nail That Holds All

The Cross and the Issue of Meaning

ou are a king, then!" said Pilate. Jesus answered, "You are right in saying I am a king. In fact, for this reason I was born, and for this I came into the world, to testify to the truth. Everyone on the side of truth listens to me."

"What is truth?" Pilate asked. With this he went out again to the Jews and said, "I find no basis for a charge against him" (John 18:37–38 NIV).

When Pilate asked Jesus, "What is truth?" his question went unanswered—at least Christ gave him no verbal answer. Jesus' silence may have come because he realized that Pilate was really asking, "Why am I upon this planet?"

This plaintive question always comes from a deep hunger for life's meaning. It is every suicide's question up to the very moment the lips taste the steel of the cold gun barrel. If the despairing could only find meaning in existence, they would not hesitate to go on living. Baffled over Pilate's question, "What is truth?" they are met by a groaning silence. Which of us has not stared into the ashen, empty face of human existence and cried, "Father, who are we? Why are we here?" Which of us has not wept that we doubted God or tried to find some evidence that humanity was anything more than a pointless ache in the universe? We must have a reason to live, indeed we must have a reason to want to. How true the proverb that those of us who know the "why" of living can put up with any "how."

Pilate must have ached over his own lack of inner meaning when he saw Jesus affirming his kingship on the brink of death. He must have envied Jesus' confidence at knowing why he was on the planet, at seeing great purpose in the death he must endure. Jesus was silent, not because he didn't know the answer to Pilate's question, but because he knew the answer could only be revealed by dying. It could not be revealed by mere words.

So, on that night, Jesus laid both his teachings and himself on the cross and answered the issue of "why?" History is nailed together! Literally it is! The story of man, from its beginning to the present, is so varied and disconnected that it had to be nailed together to give it continuity. Ever since the nail was driven, the human story reads more smoothly. Since then, there is a vital interrelatedness between its widely separated parts. Since then, we who choose to bear his cross know why we're on the planet. We have stared into the face of the Medusa and won. There is no "why" question for us. No wonder our lives are God's great *Gloria!* No wonder the apostle tells us, "Speak to one another with psalms, hymns and spiritual songs. Sing and make music in your heart to the Lord" (Eph. 5:19 NIV). The cross answers discordant emptiness with music.

After Jesus was tried before Pilate, he met the hammer man. We will never know the name of the man who used the hammer that day. We know he was a state employee. Ignorant of his own vital role in history, he drove the nail through the hand of a man and into a cross behind it. He was so completely lost in his bloody business that he took no time to scratch his name upon the wood; so we cannot know him. We can neither congratulate him for the meaning he gave to history nor condemn him for the crucifixion of an innocent man.

✠ ✠ ✠

But looking back over history, we know that it is almost always the guilty who crucify the innocent, the terminally ill who would execute their last physician. Yet, in a real sense, we do know the one who drove the nails. Have you not seen him in your dressing-room mirror? Does he or she not gawk back from the glass like a Pharisee at an execution, thanking God that he is not as other men? It is only when we see the face of the hammer man and know it for our own that we shed our best, most honest tears. The nails were ours to hammer, not his. The bloody wood was ours, too. It's as though we gave Christ our cross to saw the timbers into lumber to build the very pulpit he used to call us to his Father. For only in the presence of his Father can we sort through the issue of meaning.

But Calvary was not our giving tree where we gave God anything of value. God was the giver there, and we the joyous takers. There we sucked from the marrow of divinity the knowledge that we are here by appointment and for a reason. Knowing the cross as our benefactor, therefore, we must not be too hard on this nameless executioner. Could he really be expected to understand the significance of the nails? After all, he had spiked six hands to crosses that dismal morning in spring. Four of those hands belonged to local hooligans, convicted by the courts of sedition and treason, and capital crimes deserve capital punishment.

So, with an "innocence" at least as great as ours, he drove the critical nail of history. <u>A hammer man only drives the nails where the state says to drive them.</u> Not even the cleverest of magistrates can look at a man's hands and pronounce him innocent or guilty; certainly not a menial state employee. So he is not really at fault. The hands of robbers and carpenters all look alike; thus, for him, the nail was driven and forgotten. <u>But not for us.</u>

✠   ✠   ✠

For us the dwindling rays of human intellect and light focus on the cross, asking, like someone being wakened from a deep sleep, "What does this mean?" The people who know have never been historians. Oddly enough, the first to know were fishermen, revenue collectors, peasants, and prostitutes who had somehow through his dying become respectable. These sorts of souls wrote the Gospels, those all-inclusive biographies of Christ, whose mini-stories begin the New Testament and widen the cast

18

of players until all of us are in the mob scene crying "Crucify!"

It is right that we have trusted their report. In the first century the apostles were the needy who knew him. Now we are the needy whose greatest need is to know him. They were the old generation of beggars who packaged the bread of salvation for our generation. We eat from their recipe of life—real life that knows why it lives and thus knows meaning.

I have asked the Father that I might never forget that these who first trusted the cross were my brothers and sisters. They have called him Lord in centuries gone by, that I might call him Lord in mine. They stood at the cross, drinking its life so long ago, then crooked a finger to beckon me to that glorious place where I could be reborn. So I have found a Savior and an altar where I might sacrifice all my little reasons to live and gain a bigger reason to "be."

Those men of old were generally all uneducated pariahs—men of no status. Yet, they began to insist very noisily that the eighteenth year of Emperor Tiberius was history's most important year, for it was the Year of the Cross. It was God's year for answering humanity's most fundamental issue: "Why am I on this planet?" Those who first believed could not be hushed! They shouted it from dungeon windows and prison stocks. They were buried beneath piles of stones thrown in anger. Their heads rolled. Ironically, some were crucified in their defense of the crucifixion. And to what have these martyrs (or "witnesses," for that is what the word *martyr* means) called us? To Sunday's cafeteria-style churches, where we select the worship we want to hear? To committee quarrels, where our prosaic egos lobby for control within Christ's body of believers? God forbid!

19

⊥⊦ ⊥⊦ ⊥⊦

These who would not change their minds about the cross, and refused to change the subject, called us to their own private Calvarys and, more importantly, to ours as well. Gradually they triumphed! Ever so slowly, as they convinced the world that the central event in time and eternity was the cross, they bade us turn from our naive discipleship. They understood that the sporadic graph of history reached its zenith in the year twenty-seven, the Year of the Cross. That year our nameless benefactor took his hammer and fastened together our meaningless, disconnected story. Oh, how we yet need this nail to spike our own short lives to something more enduring.

It is this part of the cross' power over humanity's meaningless story that draws me to it. It holds sway over my story, too. Poets and composers have raised the cross to the center of art and literature, but need and hunger have raised it at the center of our lives. We need some human being to cry "I love you!" in such a way that leaves no question that he or she really means it.

When I was nine years old, I heard the cross preached in such a way that I knew I was loved. My childhood was there marked with a sense of awe. The *titulus*—that I.N.R.I. sign above the cross—for me read only "Abba." I had a Father and he had two sons. His only begotten Son purchased meaning and gave it, wrapped in thorns, to me, the son he had lately adopted (Rom. 8:15).

You will never see the cross as the center of your own history until you see it as the center of all history. Other pieces of human events may seem to you to have deeper meaning for man's existence. You might name the Code of Hammurabi, or the Decalogue, or the Magna Carta, as of equal importance. The year 27 might not be as significant to you as 44 B.C., or 1066, or 1588, or even 1945. Yet none of these events has been as fundamental to fulfilling all human meaning as the cross. We are but the momentary children of all millennia. Since we cannot live long on earth, we must hurriedly ask the vital life questions. They are not new questions. Men from the Stone Age to the Space Age have been vexed in lonely moments by only a few great questions: "Where have I come from?" "Where am I going?" "What's the use of my being here?" The cross has answered.

The cross replies splendidly and clearly for us while secular historians poke through their musty old annals in a futile attempt to find the answers. Of course, they are not to be found in secular chronicles. Such history can inform us; it cannot keep our souls alive. So human genius from Socrates to Schopenhauer did not have the answers. None of the tyrants from Hannibal to Hitler had them. But somewhere between Nebuchadnezzar and Napoleon, there was a Nazarene who did.

If these are more than matter-of-fact questions in our lives, they require more than matter-of-fact replies. We are hungry for hope. We are dying and want to live on. As we face the great question mark of death, we plead, "O God, give us no words! There are too many writers already. Give us something that transcends talk. Let us see the answers in something as visible as the blood of Yahweh dripping on the steel head of a crucifier's hammer. Perhaps then we can live." A great ballet artist, on completion of a masterful interpretation, was asked why she performed the dance that particular way. "If I could have said it, do you suppose I would have danced it?" she replied. So it was with Christ. He would not have answered us with a cross if he could have answered us with his lips and made us understand.

These answers could not be spoken; they had to be suffered. They were all laid bare for us on the cross. They were developed in three days of darkness, while men and women argued with themselves as to what his sacrifice had meant. Then, with the emergence of that first Easter, man's deepest longings had been fulfilled. The fundamental issues all had answers. Yet we still argue.

✠   ✠   ✠

How are these basic questions related to history, and how is our personal history related to the cross? History is more than the progression of events and dates. It is composed of men who get hungry, curse the light, love, weep, and sometimes die in convulsion and pain. So it is correct to say that the Battle of Salamis was fought in 480 B.C. It is correct, but not very adequate.

It seems to me there are three modes of history. There is the remote history we read about. The Battle of Salamis is that. But we should be aware that beneath the surface reporting is the real pain of history. At Salamis there were Greek children snatched from the combat area. Some were killed in the process, and their mothers fell to asking all those vital questions. There were Athenian lads who had never killed a man, trying desperately to find some justification for what they were asked to do. There was crusty old Xerxes, who watched as the smaller Grecian navy outmaneuvered his great Persian fleet. Knowing the pain of failure, all the questions came to him, too.

There is a second mode of history—that which is recent and touches our lives. Iwo Jima is such history for me. I was seven years old when that battle was fought. I lived in a small Oklahoma town. Still, it is history in which our little community participated. We sent the finest, most debonair and handsome young man in our neighborhood to participate in that history. He came back on a hospital ship, twisted, crippled, and spastic. He never married. Certainly similar questions have come to him: "Where have I been?" "Why me?" "Where will I end up?" And, of course, history with its muted volumes stands silent.

The third mode of history is our own current immersion in the vast everydayness of life. We are all immersed in this contemporary history. We are living in the Year of the Test-Tube Baby, or the Drought in Ethiopia or the Mid-East Crisis. Television's nightly news has brought us an awareness of history being made hour by hour. "One hundred men died in this riot," we hear a commentator say; or, "There was heavy fighting in that area"; or, "It was the greatest air tragedy of the year to date." They are facts that link us in the present to the endless history of human heartbreak. Still, if these events do not seem directly to involve us, we often stake them out on the edge of consciousness and try to forget about them.

A more personal involvement occupies the very center of our attention. We live secularly. If we live in a city, we are the urban urbane. Or we become involved with some civic associations to gain status. We are presidents of bowling leagues or are working on our "Who's Who" certificates. If one of our lodge brothers doesn't blackball us, we will soon be a "Cobra" in the "Royal Order of the Mongoose." Finally, there is that dollar-a-year charities board to which we were elected; frankly, it is not worth all the headaches, but it does get us an invitation to the governor's ball.

This is our micro-history! It sews up our time by demanding that we paint posters or stuff tissue in the chicken-wire frame for the club's homecoming float. While we love these involvements, there still come times when, like an actor worn out from rehearsal, we wonder if the drama is worth it. Then those plaguing questions come flying out of the darkness to haunt us. Despite all the energy we have been expending, we feel a lack of depth and achievement. We have been busy—no doubt about that—but it is a squirrel-cage frenzy that gets us nowhere.

Trapped by the unimportant kind of history we are making, we have, perhaps, two ways out. There is the aspirin bottle, which will at best only postpone the questions. Or there is the cross of Christ, which was driven like a wedge into history for history's own sake. It does not simply brush the questions aside for the present; it answers them. It is God's best antidote for our own unsatisfying participation in the human struggle.

✠   ✠   ✠

Perhaps the cross answers our conflicts because, too, it is steeped in conflict. For two hundred decades now, men have crawled out of every little corner of time to throw rocks at the cross. Philosophers have pelted it with laughter, asking its purpose, but the cross has answered them in the words of Paul, one of its greatest old defenders: "The preaching of the cross is to them that perish foolishness; but unto us which are saved it is the power of God" (1 Cor. 1:18 KJV).

The logicians have cried that the message of the cross is too unbelievable for the educated or the wise, but the cross has answered again: "Where is the wise? where is the scribe? where is the disputer of this world? hath not God made foolish the wisdom of this world?" (1 Cor. 1:20 KJV).

Has the cross successfully answered its critics? Well, they are mostly all gone now, and it remains in place. It

24

has outlived all its assailants to bring to us new meaning and to set our feet on a pathway that leads somewhere important. It would like to do this for the whole world at once, but that is not the way of the cross. It builds its belief one heart at a time. It enlists its army soldier by soldier. But it confronts us all, fearing neither us nor the whole of history.

The cross is there to remind us that we have come from God. It was he who created us in his image. Just think of it! We have come from God, and we are made like him intellectually, morally, and spiritually. God is that great power who made us with the ability to choose, hoping we would be strong enough to choose the right course.

But the cross, too, has come from God. It has come because we were created good and have gone bad. Given the power to choose between sin and righteousness, we chose sin. However, we need not despair over this lack of righteousness in our lives. The cross has such mystical but certain logic that all men and women—all who have lived their lives without goodness or purpose—may accept its immaculate righteousness and its depth of meaning.

✠   ✠   ✠

But what has this tree of execution to do with righteousness in our lives? Everything! Because the man who died there did so only after thirty-three years of perfect existence. Year after year he met each of the commandments without a single violation. He was tempted to commit every sin in the thesaurus of human iniquity; yet he never committed one. He was indeed "tempted in every way, just as we are—yet was without sin" (Heb. 4:15 NIV).

The cross has become the symbol of his sinless righteousness. It was because he clung so tightly to his righteousness that he ever faced the cross. Christ could have avoided his death by surrendering his sinlessness. For instance, when the Roman magistrate asked him if he was a king, he could have said, "No, I am a humble carpenter!" and avoided the cross. When the priests asked him if he was the Son of God, he could have said, "Why, the very idea is ridiculous!" and again he could have avoided the cross. But to have answered thus would have been lying, for Jesus knew that he was both the Son of God and the King of Jews. So he refused to lie about it. He laid hold of truth and refused to abandon it, even to save his life.

At Calvary, truth died, holding out its bloody hands to falsehood. So has come a chain of men and women two thousand years long, asking Christ to take the fullness of righteousness that was his and place it in the center of their lives. The promise is now extended to us. Though we have tried to live without sin and have failed, there is yet a measure of happiness. Although we cannot depend on our own righteousness to save us, his righteousness is dependable and has already purchased our salvation.

✝   ✝   ✝

Is it not time to raise the cross in the middle of our lives? We must be careful before we answer. His cross will not coexist with our present way of life. We may not raise the cross yet ignore it in all our petty social involvements. Once we salute it momentarily we must serve it hourly for the rest of our lives. The cross is the supreme example of righteousness and can never belong to the person who will not show it supreme respect.

God has placed the cross in history. From Adam to the atom, people have found contingency in that cross. Just as history's finest hour was the hour of Calvary, so our greatest moment will be that small quantum of time when we say with Paul, "The preaching of the cross is to them that perish foolishness; but unto us which are saved it is the power of God."

The crucifixion invites us to complete the cycle of human failure and redemption. Each of us is created by God. Then, without exception, each of us moves away from the righteousness in which we were created. Then comes his invitation, issued by his cross, to return by way of Christ's sacrifice to fellowship with our Father and savor everlasting life. Years ago I wrapped my own search for meaning in these sixteen lines.

> Poor souls, we are without purpose,
> From battle to battle we run,
> We are orphans who nervously search
> For a Father to call us his sons.
>
> Anxiety throbs in our heads
> Our mind tries some purpose to see,
> There's a strange, empty vacuum of pain
> In the place where our hearts ought to be.
>
> There can yet be life for the lifeless.
> The hopeless have one hope sublime;
> For our Master has driven His cross
> In the cascading decades of time.
>
> Come let us move from the foment of life,
> And refine all the gold from the dross,
> And fasten our purposeless living
> To God's wondrous assurance, the cross.

The hands of Christ
seem very frail

For they were broken
by a nail.

But only they
reach heaven at last

Whom these frail,
broken hands
hold fast.

John R. Moreland

2

The Wood of the New Agreement

The Cross and the Issue of Salvation

*N*ow it was the day of Preparation, and the next day was to be a special Sabbath. Because the Jews did not want the bodies left on the crosses during the Sabbath, they asked Pilate to have the legs broken and the bodies taken down. The soldiers therefore came and broke the legs of the first man who had been crucified with Jesus, and then those of the other. But when they came to Jesus and found that he was already dead, they did not break his legs. Instead, one of the soldiers pierced Jesus' side with a spear, bringing a sudden flow of blood and water (John 19:31–34 NIV).

"We must kick the darkness 'til it bleeds daylight," cried Bruce Cockburn.[1] In a similar manner, Dylan Thomas advised us: "Do not go gentle into that good night . . . Rage, rage against the dying of the light."[2] Both poets here sing the story of the cross: our salvation. Jesus on Good Friday kicked the darkness till it bled light; indeed, he raged against the dying of the light till he purchased for us the entire realm of light. And so we are saved! I bow my head and bend my knee before this mighty carpenter-conqueror. At death and even before, two roads diverge. Hell lies down one and heaven up the other, and where the turnpike splits, hangs the God-man who illuminates my choice of destinies. I daily stop, like Bunyan's Pilgrim, and look up into that faithful, thorn-ringed face. I cannot look too long, for just the shortest glance causes me to lower my eyes and beg him answer grace's greatest question: "Is all of this for me?"

I'm disturbed that the "why" of Calvary is so untroubling to the masses. If Jesus had been crucified in our day, doubtless the press release would have gone something like this:

United Press International
The United Arab Republic announced by repeated broadcast on Radio Cairo that Jesus Bar Joseph was executed for inciting riots and aiding in insurrection. His repeated inferences that he was some sort of king or leader seemed to be a threat to the national and international stability of many Near Eastern countries. His execution seemed unprotested even by his closest followers. Officials in Tel Aviv felt that Jesus, who only days earlier had caused a riot in Jerusalem, might be planning a military coup. Although no specific charge has as yet been released concerning his execution, it is generally known that he was openly

unsympathetic with the present political regime of that
country.

Then, of course, this dispatch would have been followed by a half-dozen other reports of various world trouble spots. All the smart new words that have been added
to the glossary of political science would be used—*uni-
lateral, junta, cease-fire, aggressor, disarmament, provoca-
tive, imperialist*. This would be followed by local news,
weather, and sports. Then, after a sandwich and a glass of
milk, we and our fellow Americans would turn off our TVs
and go to bed. It is sad that we have weaned ourselves
from our sense of need. We sleep before the cross untrou-
bled because we have congratulated all the sin out of our
lives. We have "self-esteemed" ourselves into the court
of God, and now we sit at tea with the Almighty and never
notice that we are "wretched, pitiful, poor, blind and
naked" (Rev. 3:17 NIV). How well we've learned to accept
ourselves.

Here is our culture's blasé lack of concern about the
cross. Blinded by the glaucoma of the new narcissism, we
no longer see the cross' relevance or significance. There is
such an abundance of human conflict and suffering in
today's world that the cross, were it to happen now, would
seem to us far more categorical than unique. Why should
we get too excited about one man on one cross when over
a hundred people were killed in yesterday's air tragedy,
thousands were gunned down in Desert Storm so recently,
and millions are dying of starvation today? No, to our
own poor video-glazed eyes, the cross may simply be a
minor tragedy, of little import in our self-important lives.

Is the cross truly the juncture between heaven and hell?
One dominant metaphor of the Exodus is Moses' lifting up
the brazen serpent on a pole to the Israelites who had

31

been bitten by serpents of rebuke (Num. 21:6–9). In the cross, God stands it up again in our very midst. To merely look is to live. Looking seems so small a price to pay for life. But there hangs the crude brass snake and that odd command, "Look and live!" Our pride is the great deterrent—our refusal to admit we are in need. Fang-marked and invenomed with death, the masses glance everywhere else except at their only hope. But we who know our poverty and need, know that our living lies in looking.

☩   ☩   ☩

I never will forget that first plain Pentecostal service I attended as a boy. The evangelist—a rural Oklahoma icon of red weathered skin and fervent emotion—preached on the cross. I now know he likely melodramatized the event, but it is to his credit that for the first time in my young life I saw that all nine years of my transgression was part of the crushing agony that slew my greatest lover. I had been bitten in a mortal way, but the brazen serpent of the cross hung in hopeful, heavy coils that drew the venom from my life and cleansed me in but a single look. The cross remains as vivid for me now as it did in that first saving glimpse. My world was as small then as Garfield County, Oklahoma. Yet, believe me when I say that I knew—somehow—that the cross was cosmic. I was overwhelmed by its gargantuan size and by my vision of the skully hill where Jesus died for me.

Now I know grace for its true glory. Then I knew that Golgotha was not in Garfield County, nor did Jesus die in any time close to mine. But when I saw all those rustic Oklahoma saints weeping over his death, I knew I must weep, too, for this was bigger and more sweeping in its importance than anything I could imagine.

Years later I would learn that German theologism *Heils-geschicte*, "saving history," and I would understand that history could be recounted in two ways. Its story could be told totally in terms of man's time on the earth, or it could be told in terms of God's never-ending pursuit of man on the earth. And how he does pursue us, as Francis Thompson wrote so long ago:

> I fled Him, down the nights and down the days;
> I fled Him, down the arches of the years;
> I fled Him, down the labyrinthine ways
>   Of my own mind; and in the mist of tears
> I hid from Him, and under running laughter.
> Up vistaed slopes, I sped;
>   And shot, precipitated.
> Adown Titanic glooms of chasmed fears.
> From those strong Feet that followed, followed after.[3]

Yes, the feet follow after—wounded feet they are, too—crucified feet. God is indeed the Hound of Heaven who pursues each of us through our particular corridor of time. One by one, he tracks us down until, seized by this loving God, we poor humans are made rich by a single look that enables us to live. I became caught up by the idea that I was "saved by the blood," as we were prone to "testify."

✠   ✠   ✠

In a way all new young believers are children and yet Jesus said, "Allow them to come to me, for of such is the kingdom of God" (Matt. 19:14). Why such praise for the naive? Because the cross finds fertile socket in the tenderness of those who raise it in honor while it is virtually ignored by those who arrogantly feel themselves intellectually mature. Jesus knew that while theologians may speak only academically of *Heilsgeschicte,* the simple heart of a child thrills at the conquering work of God.

> Sing above the battle strife—
> Jesus saves! Jesus saves!
> By his death and endless life—
> Jesus saves! Jesus saves![4]

And so it was that long ago I joined those who sang in a very small clap-sided, one-room church about an event so cosmic in its power that it ransoms all of us.

✠　　✠　　✠

How big is the cross event? Large enough to shadow all history: human history and my history. One Hebrew word would teach me all its glory: *yasha.* This word, I learned a decade later, means "salvation"—it really means "to create room, to make space, as if by knocking down walls."

To look is not just to live, but to thrive in a wall-less world. Here is the glory of the cross; it bludgeons ghettos, removes fences, and erases boundaries. It calls all littleness to stare at a world large enough to permit anything. The cross saves us by pushing back the walls of prejudice and small thinking. It saves us by pushing back the stockades of narrow ego. It flattens our Jerichos until we stand blinking in the brightest sunlight to be imagined. The cross is theological salvation, but it is also sociological and psychological salvation. When I am prone to hate others or condemn them, I hear Paul saying, "Who is he that condemns? It is Christ that died" (Rom. 8:34). This is where my sickly sociology is made well, where my over-egotistic psychology waits to follow, and where, for the sake of my own pastoral reputation, I see the dying Savior and know that I must be crucified with Christ to live (Gal. 2:20).

But the cross is not just to spare me the tinyness of my own poor reputation. The cross is the look-and-live event that saves my days as it saves my soul. Because of my own crucified living, I can redeem the time. I save the very years of my service as a present unto God. Further, I see time as that commodity that is limited for me but never for him. God stood the cross in the center of time as we see it, but for God it stands above all time, redeeming every second of every millennium.

✙   ✙   ✙

The crucifixion is now over by two thousand years. But in those centuries that preceded it, God sent a vanguard of prophets to announce its arrival. None of these preachers overlooked its importance. Jeremiah, without mentioning the cross, clearly outlined its benefits:

> Behold, the days come, saith the LORD, that I will make a new covenant with the house of Israel . . . this shall be the covenant that I will make with the house of Israel . . . I will put my law in their inward parts, and write it in their hearts; and will be their God, and they shall be my people (Jer. 31:31–33 KJV).

The cross, as Jeremiah saw it, is God's new covenant. It is Yahweh's new agreement. It is God's "new deal."

What was the "old deal" that God had given to us? Well, he has a yardstick graduated from one to ten. Listed by each of the graduations is one of his commandments, which he asks us to keep inviolate. The graduations are perfectly calibrated and exact. There is absolutely nothing wrong with his yardstick. The problem is that we are too short. Nobody measures up.

But somewhere in that mystical presence that is the mind of God there existed a plan to measure us differently. Oh, he would use the yardstick, to be sure. But he would lay before that yardstick a cross on which he, through the miracle of incarnation, had died. Then every one of us who stood on the cross would be so elevated that we could measure up to the top of God's expectations. It would not be because we had gained any moral and spiritual height, but simply because God would allow us to gain the added stature we need for acceptance by standing on the cross.

Paul points out our glorious new stature! ". . . no one," he says, "will be declared righteous in his sight by observing the law . . . for all have sinned and fall short of the glory of God, and are justified freely by his grace through . . . a sacrifice of atonement, through faith in his blood . . ." (Rom. 3:20–25 NIV). To measure up is wonderful! We have been saved not by the Ten Commandments that we could never keep, but by the cross that keeps *us* and presents us faultless [without sin] and with great joy to our Savior (Jude 24–25).

✠ ✠ ✠

But what does this really mean—this standing on the cross to gain stature? It means that in the greatness of this drama we learn our true size. We are not to see his cross as titanic and ourselves as but worms—as some theologians once taught—but we are to see our neediness and the immensity of God. At the cross, humility is a natural garment. At the cross, we need not try to reduce our importance by sighing, "Oh, to be nothing, nothing." Rather, we have only to stand next to the magnificence of Christ, and our own moral shabbiness will be instantly obvious. Humility is never self-depreciation. It is but gaining the true view of who we are as we catch a first glimpse of his finished majesty. Then, like the centurion, we cry, "Surely this was the Son of God!" (Matt. 27:54), and at the same time we cry, "Surely this is me!" And like the teenage Isaiah, we cry honestly, "Woe is me, for I am lost! I am a man of unclean lips" (Isa. 6:5).

And to whom do we give thanks for these new insights into ourselves? Unto our crucified Savior. This is God's "new deal." This is God's deliberate and refined plan: his fine-tuned historical way of helping us. We must never feel that Jesus simply got caught in the political machinery of his day and was crushed in the gears. The cross was not an accident. It was not a tragedy that surprised God; it was one he anticipated.

✠ ✠ ✠

Some time ago in New York City, a man was trying to board a subway with his wife. In the rush and hurry of the busy hour, she stepped quickly into one of the coaches of the train. Her husband, pushing and shoving to get in, didn't quite make it. The door of the train closed on his arm. Try as he might, he could not free his arm from the locked door. Then he shuddered as he felt the brakes release and the train lurch. His wife, seeing his condition, began screaming. She could neither free his arm from the door nor get the train stopped.

The poor man tried in vain to anchor himself to something on the station platform. As the train pulled away, he began running, but only at the very first was he able to keep up with the train. In a terrible, horrible instant, the coach in which his arm was caught was flogging him at rapid speeds against the concrete abutments of the subway tube. The train stopped too late. The man died, accidentally caught in the press of people, all going somewhere unimportant. The event got only spotted news coverage.

To most, it was a tiny tragedy of little significance. The underground trains stopped only long enough to carry the man from the tunnel. Then once again they rattled and banged their way through those infinite miles of sunless tubes. One little man among tens of thousands who ride the iron serpents had accidentally been killed by a malfunctioning machine.

✠ ✠ ✠

We may be prone to view the cross in this way. We may see Jesus as one little man accidentally trapped in the mechanism of Hebrew custom and Roman politics. Such is not the case. The cross was programmed exactly as it happened, and all for us. And, mysteriously and wonderfully, without ever knowing the program, Herod, Pilate, and the mob followed it. Jesus truly was "the Lamb slain before the foundation of the world" (Rev. 13:8). There was nothing haphazard or accidental about his cross. The cross was accomplished by blueprints that were older than this world—blueprints carefully drafted and meticulously scheduled and detailed. The cross was a planned project that God deliberately offered to save us.

The cost of the project was immense. Its expense was so great that now the greatest sin we may commit is to try to measure up to God's expectation without the advantage of the cross. We cannot treat the cross with the same momentary interest with which we receive a late-wire news report. The cross is more than a casual item in our well-being. It is life and death—eternal life and eternal death. The cross is for us the wood and fiber of God's new agreement.

God's new agreement promises that we all may now come home to him, but we must come by the way of the cross. There is no other way to God. All other roads, however clearly marked, lead only to the "Slough of Despond" or to "Vanity Fair."

> Jesus, keep me near the cross—
> There a precious fountain,
> Free to all, a healing stream,
> Flows from Calv'ry's mountain.[5]

✠ ✠ ✠

The cross, and it alone, is dramatic and bold enough to save us. There is no way to God that does not depend on nails, thorns, ropes, and wood. There, where the soldiers gambled over garments and the priests mocked a dying carpenter, is the very place where God makes his agreement with us.

Vengeance was there robed in spite and retaliation. Judas may have been retaliating because he felt that Jesus liked the other apostles more than him. The Romans were retaliating because they hated all Jews. The Pharisees hated Jesus, for he struck out at their hypocrisy. The Sadducees hated him, for he drew people away from their doctrines. The Herodians feared him, for they misunderstood the nature of his kingship.

So their lust for vengeance burned against Jesus. It was their Gordian knot of human pettiness that bound him to his cross: that "get even" desire that Adam passed on to all of us. It was that same desire that had kept Esau lying in wait for his brother Jacob for years. It was the same spirit of vengeance that the young David held in his heart when he slew the giant oppressor of his people. It was the one dream of sightless old Samson grinding in the prison house, dreaming in darkness of the day when he would avenge Philistia for the last time.

Paul strongly rebuked the Corinthians for coming to that cross-enriched symbol called communion and hating and quarreling beneath love's finest ensign, the cross (1 Cor. 11:17–22). Hate is the great antithesis of the cross. Love is the only human emotion that may traffic the *Via Dolorosa*.

⚜ ⚜ ⚜

Only once in my life have I been hated by another Christian (before you see this as paranoia, please hear this out). I generally feel that most Christians may be petty in their goodwill from time to time. But only once have I felt the base force of hatred directed toward me. It was chilling! Yet much more than that hate abused the suffering Christ, as heartless anger and blind hostility were hurled at him from all directions.

A few times I have seen Christians caught up in vendettas of ugliness and hatred one for another. Always I weep for their blind ignorance of their dying lover. While salvation is the loss of walls, hate constructs those walls again over the remnants of old ego whose shattered pieces are kept too close at hand.

Grudge and bitterness defile the saving work of Christ. I well remember a woman whose ill will toward a sister led her ultimately to a savage burglary of her hated sister's home. Once inside the home, she destroyed property and defaced family portraits. To what extent will bitterness track hate? Hebrews 12:15 says that it will destroy all his precious dying work.

The cross deals with malice because it was raised in the center of human hate. How did Jesus react to this united spirit of hate? He forgave! And then from the cross he offered God's "new deal" to a thief and a Roman legionary. Hate had scourged love. Hate had ringed love with thorns. Hate had pierced, torn, and mocked love. But love won! It continues to win! There love hangs, loving the haters, dying for the assassins, caring for the unconcerned, bleeding for the unwounded.

✠   ✠   ✠

The blood of Christ is the witness of God to the triumph of love. The blood of Christ is God's signature on his new agreement with us. The blood means that God means business and the agreement is valid. God asks only that we look on the cross and believe his agreement. Once in my journal, near Eastertime, I wrote:

Can you hear it dripping crimson?
Splashing color into a vivid world?
Dripping warmth over a frigid social system?
Dripping life into the walking corpses
Of the twentieth-century's aching vacuum?
Steadily it falls from the massive wooden beams of the
     cross;
Two hundred decades have not arrested its incessant flow;
Tyrants and wars have not plugged the supply;
Steadily it drips in a divine rhythm of redemption.
Stop Niagara if you must!
But you will never stop the drops of eternal love;
They will flow while one heart yet knows how to hate.

The cross proves that God does mean business. God is in earnest. With the seriousness of Gethsemane, he offers

41

us this new agreement. But an agreement is never established by just one party. An agreement is the meeting of two minds. The agreement is not completed when God offers us life through the cross, but only when we accept it.

Too long there has been a "So what?" attitude of acceptance about the cross. We are never to see the cross as merely another story with a poor ending. Calvary is the place where God made a new agreement with us. The agreement is not imaginary. It is as substantial as the fiber of the cross itself. God was deadly serious when he offered us this agreement. Golgotha is not a Bavarian passion play where the actors mimic the final chapters of the Book of Matthew and charge us so much per seat. It is God, caught up in the violence of life and death, who extends to us the benefits of Christ's sufferings. This new agreement is a life-and-death business, and wise are we to consider it such.

Essentially, this new covenant is God saying, "I want your life for the life of my Son." It is a life-for-life agreement; we should be willing to give God all that we have, since God gave us all that *he* had. We must not consider how much it will cost to participate in the agreement, for he did not count the cost. We are to learn obedience unto him, even as the Son obeyed his Father.

✠   ✠   ✠

Here at the cross, all the issues are drawn in superlatives. God will cut no deals with us for half a life. He will not bargain on proportionate dedication. With him it is either all or nothing. If we are not prepared to offer him everything, we must not waste our time offering him anything. If we are ever to discover the joy of God's new agreement, we must come to him with this kind of prayer:

Dear Lord of the New Agreement,

They are yours—these hands of mine that have dipped in the mire of sin, these feet of mine that have too long walked in their own way.

Here, Lord! Accept these lips that have dealt so often in lies and curses.

Is this heart of mine so hardened by spiritual sclerosis that it cannot beat in soft compassion?

I bring you so little. I'm such an imperfect piece of clay, but the whole mold is yours, God!

Let everyone say there isn't much, but let no one say it isn't all.

Dearest God, if you can love this desperate piece of your world, then all of me is yours for your own pleasure.

Thank you for the cross and the peace of the new agreement.

*Thou didst not come down
from the cross when they
shouted to thee, mocking
and reviling thee,*

*"Come down from the cross
and we will believe that
Thou art He."*

*Thou didst not come down,
for again Thou wouldst not
enslave men by a miracle,
and didst crave faith freely
given, not based on miracle.*

Feodor Dostoevsky
The Grand Inquisitor

3

The Timbers of Grief

The Cross Answers Our Grieving

Near the cross of Jesus stood his mother, his mother's sister, Mary the wife of Clopas, and Mary of Magdala. When Jesus saw his mother there, and the disciple whom he loved standing nearby, he said to his mother, "Dear woman, here is your son," and to the disciple, "Here is your mother." From that time on, this disciple took her into his home (John 19:25–27 NIV).

Once on a tree there was a man. Over the tree were the bold letters of a sign, announcing in three languages the heresy that had ordered his suffering. Beneath the tree was the mother of the heretic. She was a woman whose face was rimmed by little wisps of gray hair that protruded

45

defiantly from under her mantle; occasionally she trembled with uncontrollable spasms of grief. Before the tree stood a young fisherman whose broad arm cradled the head of the accursed man's mother. He was unable to offer her consolation—the man on the cross was her son. But he could offer her his strong young arm, which rippled with the very kind of strength that could sustain a mother forced to see her son on the gallows.

When Michelangelo carved his *Pietà*, he carved Mary two-thirds larger than she should have been. Why? Because he envisioned her as giantesque, holding her executed son with the largesse of a dowager queen in the wrenching contemplation of death. The exact opposite is really true. Grief does not enlarge us, it diminishes us.

The real Mary is grieving and feels destroyed by the crucifixion herself. Perhaps she is also remembering Simeon's words of prophecy, spoken to her years ago when the infant Jesus had been brought to the Jerusalem temple for the purification required by Jewish law: "And a sword will pierce your own soul too" (Luke 2:35b NIV). The word Simeon used is the Greek *romphaia*, a huge Persian sword that literally skewers its victims in pain.

Grief is always a *romphaia* in our lives. I remember a neighbor woman whose son had been a chum of mine. The boy had shocked us all by being involved in a terrible crime, for which he was sentenced to prison. On the day of his sentencing, I saw the sword of grief run the woman through.

✠ ✠ ✠

Likewise, here at Calvary is a pitiable trio: the dying carpenter, his sorrowing mother, and his idealistic young friend. What is there in this sort of thing that causes us to proclaim the cross the beginning of a great world faith?

Mary was not the first mother to lose a son, nor will she be the last. Is this more cosmic in meaning than the mother in our generation who receives a telegram that her only son is a casualty of war? The answer to the issue may well be connected to that sign fastened above the cross. It was much more than just a board labeled with ancient characters. It was a proclamation that distinguishes the death of Jesus from all other cases of human bereavement. "Jesus of Nazareth, King of the Jews" read the sign. The inscription was one of the claims the crucified man had made. This claim, along with others, had so angered institutional Judaism that in the spirit of unorganized rioting, it had picked up thorns, hammers, and such other ingredients of cross-making.

The inscription over the cross has transformed his dying to the great stop sign of our lives. I have confessed in the previous chapter that the cross stops *me*. It is that one great visible ensign that dominates our churches, sitting steeple-perched to challenge me with the dailyness of Luke 9:23. Am I bearing my cross, dying daily that he might live and proclaim himself sovereign over all dying? Do I care about the whole of human misery? Is his dying causing me to ask, "Who now is on some cross of political contriving?" As I consider Mary's grief I must ask whom might I console, whom might I comfort, as John comforted Mary? Christ's dying is our call to compassion.

What were the antecedents of that grief felt by Jesus' friend and Jesus' mother? Were those antecedents not his claims? The cross always reminds us that Jesus had gotten himself into trouble with the religious leaders because of what he stated to be the truth concerning his person and ministry. What does this mean for us? What were some of these claims? To begin with, we need to remember that he claimed to be without ordinary human parentage:

> The Jews then murmured at him, because he said, I am the bread which came down from heaven. And they said, Is not this Jesus, the son of Joseph, whose father and mother we know? how is it then that he saith, I came down from heaven? (John 6:41–42 KJV).

Then, too, in confidence he announced that he was the Messiah prophesied of old. He implied that he was the King of kings and would rise again on the third day after his death. Finally, there was the claim that did the most to produce his execution: He called himself the Son of God, even at his trial (Luke 22:70).

The cross was supposed to silence all his claims. It only substantiated them. Now, instead of railing at the cross with scorn, we salute it. We do not look at it through eyes of hate; we exalt it as ultimate love. We do not cry that the cross is wretched, but that *we* are. Since that fateful day, we have joined a stream of souls, two thousand years long, each apologizing to the cross for the sinful and unbelieving part of human nature that produced it. And so that rough sign, too hastily lettered with ancient glyphs, has proven true—Jesus is King! Not only does the cross validate that claim, but it is acid proof for every claim that Jesus made.

✛ ✛ ✛

So when we behold the brokenness of John and Mary, we feel their grief has come from the immediate sense of the lostness of all Jesus had promised them. They wept not just because he was dying, but that his wonderful claims were dying with him. So at least that much of their grief was wasted. His promises did not die—nor will they ever die. His resurrection turned all their grief to joy.

When we come to the cross, we are confronted with Jesus Christ and the majesty of his claims. Was he the Son of God, or was he not? Was he the Messiah, or was he mistaken? Was he the Savior, or was he self-deluded? Then suddenly it is clear to us: Either Jesus is the most vital person in all of history or he suffered from immense delusions of grandeur. There is no halfway point of resolving these extremes. There is no middle ground here for believers. We are either most wise for subscribing to his claims, or fools for revering his delusions. Where are the credentials for those things Jesus claimed? The cross alone is affirmation enough for each of them.

Jesus claimed to be God's Son. His executioners said that the very fact that he did not come down from the cross was evidence that he was not the Son of God—son of Joseph perhaps, or son of Mary, but not the Son of God (Matt. 27:43). We must admit that God is strangely silent as Jesus dies. It makes it appear as though Jesus died alone—all alone. And the loneliness of dying ever deepens our grief. Christ calls out unto God, but never does God call unto Christ. At his baptism a voice had thundered over the river, "This is my beloved Son." Such a voice at the cross would have been an answer to the cynics who questioned his sonship. But there is no voice. Jesus' unanswered cries to his Father must have seemed to some as the plaintive cry of a new orphan not yet accustomed to his parents being dead.

Crosses always seem to be places where God is silent, so we cry, "Forsaken . . . forsaken . . . forsaken! Why, God, why?" But there is only the sound of the wind and our own labored, suffocating breathing! The silence of God in our own private crucifixions gets God a lot of bad press. We're dying while the ropes chafe and the nails tear; as we cry, he retreats.

One of my friends died of cancer. As the spreading adder inside her body twisted and constricted, she lifted her eyes to her only hope of life—God. We prayed and cried, wept and entreated. But God was silent.

The mind of the skeptic indicts the silence of God even from the midst of the predicament. The words mock our Father even as they probe the quiet: "Is there no answer to your Son, God? Is it because he is not your Son? For three years now, Jesus has everywhere claimed you as his Father. Listen to his plaintive cry, 'My God, my God, why hast thou forsaken me?' [Matt. 27:46]. Will you not answer him, God? Then surely you are not his Father. His Father would not forsake him. If you do not answer your own Son, is there any chance you will answer us?" God's silence in our own need is dreadful, but his cross interprets the silence for us.

As Jesus' cry of loneliness faded into stillness, there was nothing but the whisper of morning breeze and the scream of the carrion eagles, circling effortlessly in the sky above the cross. But Jesus was more than a mere man, and his tormentors were wrong in their conclusions. There is always a time when the silence ends. There is always a time when God answers!

God in time always answers evil. He always replies to those who love foul justice. In the case of Christ, God breaks the silence, not with words but with gloom. He blotted out his sun so that "there was a darkness over all the earth until the ninth hour" (Luke 23:44 KJV). But God's darkness was not brutal—it was rather a drape of friendly shadows that helped to hide the naked shame of his beloved. Those who came in God's light to gloat victoriously over the martyrdom of Jesus would not have his light to see them home. Since the dark religious officials were so fond of making death, God confronted them with all of its uncanny horrors. In the darkness he had made to match the wickedness of human hearts, God opened graves and living dead men walked the noon gloom. Those who were bringing death to his Son met death in the streets, for men and half-men, reeking with mildew and decay, walked the marketplace and streets. Such was God's answer to the executioners of his Son: silence broken by the odd shuffling of corpses in the indistinct twilight of Christ's death.

God had one answer left for the religious leaders who felt they had done God service by raising the cross. These blind guides were supposed men of God who did not see that when they stripped Jesus and impaled him, they had attempted to steal all of God's dignity, too. In the fabulous temple, erected at great expense for his worship, God spoke with drama. The lavish draperies that hung before the Holy of Holies were indescribably beautiful, rich with color and ornate brocade. This huge valance prefaced the inner sanctum of the temple. The curtain was designed to partition the very seat of God's presence on earth—the Ark of the Covenant. These immense, heavy hangings were there to veil the holiness of God from unholy men. But as surely as if it had been old linen, God ripped the tapestries of the temple and threw them to the sides. He would not have men covering and honoring his holiness within the temple and mocking and exposing it on a hilltop outside the city.

Perhaps you find yourself asking, "Why the darkness? Why death walking as life within the city? Why the temple veil ripped angrily apart?" There are probably two reasons. God was crying, first of all. This was how God wept when his Son died unloved and alone.

The grieving God is a God whose Spirit I often invoke in the lives of those I care for. I well remember a young boy in our church who was impaled on the stiletto hood ornament of a speeding car. His death was instant. His parents were first stunned and later grieved, and finally they were hostile toward God.

"Ah," I could say to them, "do not be angry at heaven! God also lost a boy. He understands. Don't be mad at him, rather reach to him." Hebrews 12:1–3 talks of how men and women of faith look toward Jesus: the pioneer, the *archegos*, the "first-goer." When we must enter the shadow of hurt, we are relieved to see ahead of our heavy, ugly footfall the footfalls of Jesus, the *archegos* who pioneered the valley of grief.

Gethsemane's terror caused Jesus to "sweat" great drops of blood. It was not fear but grief, I think, that brought his agony. His devoted followers had fled, and he pursued their lost faithfulness with tears.

In Ephesians 4:30, the apostle Paul tells us not to grieve the Holy Spirit, with whom we are sealed to the day of redemption. Not only did Good Friday grieve the heart of the Father; God's grief continues in the current moments of our infidelity. "Grieve" is a love word. When we willfully disobey God, it is not as though we anger him, it is rather that we hurt him.

When my mother died, I felt immediately that anguish of heart that God must feel in his grief at the cross. But I could turn to God and hear him say, "Come unto me, all ye that labour and are heavy laden" (Matt. 11:28 KJV), or "Casting all your care upon him; for he careth for you" (1 Peter 5:7 KJV), or "We do not have a God who is unable to be touched with feelings of our infirmities" (Heb. 4:15).

This *archegos* God reminded me that he had been to the mourner's pyre long before me. During those dark days, the words of a wonderful hymn came to my consciousness:

Come, ye disconsolate, where'er ye languish;
Come to the mercy seat, fervently kneel;
Here bring your wounded hearts, here tell your anguish:
Earth has no sorrow that heav'n cannot heal.[1]

Why is it that heaven can heal earth's heartaches? Because God permitted himself no luxuries or easy times. He was the "first-goer" who allowed himself to know grief well ahead of us. Because God submitted his Almighty Being to the loss of his Son, we are instructed by a God who suffers.

✠   ✠   ✠

Perhaps, you say, God took it all a bit hard. He knew Jesus' suffering was only temporary. He knew that Easter would gobble up Good Friday and triumph would be eternal. Did God have to rip the temple veil and rail against the crucifiers with thunder and earthquake? But look at the Father as he reaches toward his Son. Perhaps it was only for a day or so, but the physiology of pain and death was all very real. Jesus was fully man, and his fully human nervous system was set ablaze with torture. Good fathers weep when their sons suffer.

No wonder the Book of Revelation focuses on that day when "God shall wipe away all tears from their eyes, neither shall there be any more crying" (Rev. 21:4). We grieve because something valuable has been taken away, and it is lost.

Sometimes in shopping malls our child wriggles free of us and is lost in the mall. Panic and grief seize us and we are driven to run. But in which direction? Who would know where that lost child is? Can you not see why the word *lost* is a word that grieves the heart of God? When Jesus says, "For the Son of Man came to seek and to save what was lost" (Luke 19:10 NIV), we see the dilemma of parents who are frantic over a lost child. God grieves human lostness, "not willing that any should perish" (2 Peter 3:9 KJV). God is a grieving God, and he who permitted the cross understands our grief.

⚜ ⚜ ⚜

Dr. Thomas Dooley, in his book *The Night They Burned the Mountain,* tells a correlating story that well illustrates the grief of God when we endure hopelessness or pain. One of the Laotians had given him a tiny Himalayan moonbear. It was a cuddly ball of brown fur, full of interesting antics, and Dr. Dooley set to building a cage for the animal. An old Chinese man happened upon him as he worked on the cage and stared at him in disbelief. The old man began to sob as he looked at the cage, and when Dr. Dooley sought to discover the reason for his tears, he told him that the cage was reminiscent of the greatest tragedy he had ever experienced. The old Chinese and his son had once worked together on a commune in Red China. He reminded the good doctor that laborers on the communes at harvest time were not to have one grain of rice for themselves, for it was all the property of the Republic. The son of this old man had disobeyed the harvest mandate. Since his mother was sick with beriberi and malnutrition, the son had concealed a few handfuls of rice in his clothing to take to this starving mother. He was, of course, discovered, and the authorities made a public whipping post out of the boy. They imprisoned him in a cage, not unlike the one that Dr. Dooley had made for his pet bear, and had put the caged youth in the center of the city. The cage was so small that the boy could not move or even sit up straight. The old man's testimony went like this:

> His mother and I were forced to watch, she from one side of the square and I from the other. But the guards would not allow us to go near him. Day after day, as we looked on, my boy died slowly, under the broiling sun with nothing to eat or drink, covered with filth, flies and ants. It was good when the guards pronounced him dead.[2]

The man had since escaped from China, but the very sight of cages aroused his torturous memory once more.

Again, grief was the reason for the darkness and the open graves in Jerusalem. A father was weeping over the maltreatment and brutality inflicted on his son. Tears are the way that we show our grief. But darkness was the tears and gloom was the grief of our great God, whose heart was rent by the plaintive condition of his only begotten Son and our attendant indifference.

All of our basic emotions are the way we demonstrate that we are persons—real live human beings. If we appear callous in the face of agony's great grief, others will say of us that we are inhuman. The very word *compassion* means "to suffer with." This is the phrase that is used of Jesus many times in the Gospels. Jesus was always moved with compassion. He would not let people grieve alone.

On the cross, when he says to John, "Son, behold your mother. . . . Mother, behold your son," he is saying to both of them, "Mary and John, never allow the other to suffer alone."

Do we not indeed dehumanize real live people when we are too busy to be counselors to their hurt? Paul reminds us that we should not "grieve as those who have no hope" (1 Thess. 4:13). At the base of this command lies the remembrance that we are all to bear up our entire world with a ministry to those who grieve. God is almighty in the thunder and quake of his grief at the cross.

If our compassion defines the heart of God in Christ, then what does our indifference do? "Please care!" is the cry of our alienated society. "Please care!" is the ink on every suicide note. Fifty-eight thousand Americans died in the Vietnam conflict, but a hundred thousand Vietnam veterans have committed suicide since the war ended. What was there in the hearts of those who died in battle? Why was life so distasteful to those who later killed themselves? Did they see death all around them and indifference at home?

I want to feel the Savior as he dies and the cross juts up amidst the desertion of apostles and the sparse crowd on the hilltop. I once rode on an airplane with a young man whose whole frame was shaking with sobs. I audaciously put my arm around him. It took courage, for he was a complete stranger. He told me between sobs that he was twenty years old and that every other member of his family had just been killed in an automobile accident. At the cross, God teaches us that grief should not go unattended.

There is, of course, a second reason for the unnatural display of darkness and fury that was God's response to the events of the cross. It was not merely God's sorrow. It was his power, validating Jesus' claim that God was his Father. It was, in part, God's answer to the skeptics. Those who stood by were reasoning the way of natural logic and saying, "If he is God's Son, why doesn't God do something?" So, God did something! And by those very things he did, he seemed to be saying, "I am his Father, he is my Son. All he said to you was true."

God shook his planet with an earthquake, and the rocks were split (Matt. 27:51). He shook it lightly, to be sure, for his Son had nails in his hands, and he would not bring more pain to his Son merely to answer our unbelief. He drew a veil of heavy thunderheads across the morning sun and spoke with the suddenness of crashing thunder. We still stand dumb before his power.

╬   ╬   ╬

God succeeded in validating Jesus' claim to be the Son of God. Standing near the cross was a soldier, whose daring whisper of truth was heard above the clamor of unbelieving slander. He was impressed with Jesus' meekness. He marveled at his calm even on the timbers of death. Then, when all nature seemed to invert itself and the heavens shook above the cross and the earth quaked beneath it, the soldier breathed the validity of Jesus' claim, "Truly this *was* the Son of God" (Matt. 27:54 KJV, italics added).

Here it was that life began for the centurion. When the behavior of nature was disorderly and all creation seemed topsy-turvy, a soldier made the claim for Jesus that Jesus so often had made for himself. So life began for this nameless centurion who voiced earth's conviction—Jesus is the Son of God, and God is the Mighty One who establishes creation's order, or overthrows it if he wishes.

Life—real life—always begins for us on the dark side of Calvary when we encounter the cross and affirm the centurion's statement of faith. Surely, Jesus was the Son of God. The drama of Calvary is the foundation for believing just that. Jesus was not delusional when he claimed to be the Son of God, but we are deluded if we claim to believe anything else.

Have you considered this claim? Is he Son of God, or is he not? Was the centurion right or wrong?

The reason you may not be so prone to accept what the centurion embraced as truth is that your circumstances are too different. Perhaps you confront the cross too logically in the midst of easy living. You are free to examine Golgotha in the comfort of overstuffed furniture, or while listening to the sweetness of organ music played at the church's annual Easter service. In these conditions you are undecided about it all. You are perhaps like a jeweler trying to dissect the mechanics of a timepiece. This type of analysis of the crucifixion may never lead you to say, "Surely, this was the Son of God!"

But if you were to accost it exactly as the centurion did, with the unsteady earth reeling beneath his feet and the gray sky threatening some judgment against human tyranny, you would more likely come to belief. In a split instant this soldier's heart reached out to provide ballast for his mind. His trembling lips issued the affirmation that the man on the cross was God's Son. If to no one else, at least to him, Christ was very God. The cross itself had made that clear. If it was clear to the centurion, then it must be to us. There at "the place of the skull" God stood by the assertion that Jesus so often made—he was the Son of God.

☩　☩　☩

A second possible reason for not being open to calling Jesus the Son of God is that your entire grief mechanism has never been triggered by need or pain. We cannot know what the centurion's needs were. Had he experienced grief or loss? Who can say? But grief or loss ever makes us open to calling Jesus the Son of God.

Christ made other claims that the cross certified as truth. Christ had come amongst us, calling God "Father" and teaching us that God loved us as a parent loved, only infinitely deeper. He had said early in his ministry to Nicodemus, the Hebrew statesman, "For God so loved the world, that he gave his only begotten Son, that whosoever believeth in him should not perish, but have everlasting life" (John 3:16 KJV). Did God mean it? Did he really love humanity that much? The cross says he did.

Calvary is the dilemma of divine love. God loved us, and he loved his Son. Who can measure the anguish that tore its jagged way through celestial love when God's beloved Son was on the tree? As Father, he wished to take his Son from the cross. As Creator, he dared to leave him there. It has been said that when the cross was jolted into its socket, ten thousand angels drew swords against an unfeeling planet. But God spared his precious world their wrath. Jesus had claimed God's love for us, and God demonstrated it on Good Friday.

Gethsemane was really the testing place for God's "Son-love" and God's "world-love." In the seclusion of an olive grove, the Father and his Son agreed on the final issues of deliverance for this planet earth. Although both sought to avoid the extremities of the test, there was not a minor sound anywhere in the harmony of their wills, united in the necessity of redeeming a wayward world. God assured the Son that he had to go through with the whole agony only if he wished. If he wished at any time to give it up, one cry to the Father would instantly deliver him and curse the world with eternal hopelessness and death. But the dutiful, compassionate Son, knowing his Father's love for us, set his face like a flint toward God's world-love.

Do you realize what this means? It means that God could save either us *or* his Son. Yet he and his Son together, at the expense of the Son, chose to save us. How much he must love us! It was not a detached project in which the Father was uninvolved. He felt the stigma of mockery. He, too, stumbled along the Way of Sorrows. The ghastly crown sliced at his kingship, too. He and his Son were co-sufferers. In the fondest hope that we might truly become his children, his own child died. There is no cold piece of philosophy that can do away with this. The cross is the tangible, historical evidence that God loves us. It does not say *why* God loves us, but it does answer "How much?" Paul was saying this same thing when he wrote:

> For at the very time when we were still powerless, then Christ died for the wicked. Even for a just man one of us would hardly die, though perhaps for a good man one might actually brave death; but Christ died for us while we were yet sinners, and that is God's own proof of his love towards us (Rom. 5:6–8 NEB).

Once on a tree, God proved his world-love. It was the strongest way he could say, "I love you."

✠ ✠ ✠

There is yet one other claim that the crucifixion supports. Jesus once said, "I am the way, the truth, and the life: no man cometh unto the Father, but by me" (John 14:6 KJV). What a fantastic claim! Think of the enormity of it! He did not say, "I am *a* way to God," but "I am *the* way." There is no way to God that passes by the Son, claimed Christ. This exclusivist doctrine of Christianity has led many to say that not only was Jesus deluded about himself, but he was a conceited bigot (one of the worst names one can be called in this go-along-with-it generation). This same teaching cut like a rawhide leash across the unfeeling flesh of Pharisaism. It still offends all those who seek some lesser pathway to God.

There are a thousand prophets and as many cults that outline some course of "meaningfulness" that does not involve the Christ. Some intellectuals, unable to fold the majestic claims and deeds of Jesus into their alkaline gray matter, turn to pagan mysticism or Oriental asceticism. Meanwhile, practical-minded moralists constantly measure themselves by the vague calibrations on their Golden Ruler, which they have broken and mended half-a-hundred times. Such are the pitiful attempts we make to try on our own to arrive at life's meaning. Some ultimately slash their wrists. Others become shells, whose inner emptiness is filled with the fading echoes of all that might have been.

Probably the most popular alternative to "the way of the cross" is the sincerity cult. To the devotees of this cult, doctrine is unimportant. All that matters is sincerity and "good intentions." Even the aborigine with his neck ringed in tiger teeth, if faithful to his amulet, will reach God as surely as the apostle Paul. To many, sincerity and salvation are synonyms. Ignoring the consideration that people can be sincerely wrong, sincerity says, "I may, in truth, be wrong, but Infinite Love will consider my devotion." Such self-styled religion is disgusting. No wonder some wag has said, "Be sincere, even if you don't mean it!" The sincerists, the moralists, and the hungering intellectuals are all to be pitied for their ignorance and error.

Jesus is the only way to God. May Gautama, Confucius, and Mohammed all take note. The way to God must pass through Christ and his cross. Thomas à Kempis made this same claim for Jesus:

> Follow Me: I am the way, the truth, and the life.
> Without the way there is no going;

Without the truth there is no knowing;
Without the life there is no living.[3]

But it is the cross itself that affirms this truth most clearly. The only reason the crucifixion came to be was that there were no alternatives.

If there had been any other way for us to be saved, there would never have been a Calvary. Our Lord endured the ugliness of it all, not so we might have an alternate route of redemption, but because there was no other way. Had there been some less expensive way, the Son would never have gone back to the Father with scarred hands. Nor would he ever have suffered a naked death before his mother. The grieving God is our assurance that God died to answer our needs and our grief. So often our grief is our need. If there had been any other approach possible, the Lord would have shouted the command to angelic legions, waiting at rapt attention for the call to deliver him. If the cross is anything more than the wild imaginations of the Gospel evangelists, it says emphatically, "Jesus is the Way—the only Way—the Truth and the Life."

   ✠   ✠   ✠

A fable is told of Jesus and Gabriel the archangel. It concerns the Son as he leaves the immaculate state of God's presence to hurl himself into history. Gabriel, at the last of the seven gates, arrests Christ and asks him where he is going. "To Bethlehem of Judah," answers Jesus. Gabriel seems annoyed that anyone would voluntarily leave the Crystal City for any reason, so he asks "Why?" Jesus replies that the Father loves the world and is sending him to redeem it.

Unable to turn him from his mission, Gabriel watches from the outer portal of the estate, while Jesus folds himself into flesh and is laid by a happy young mother in a manger, among the bleating of sheep and lowing of cattle. Gabriel soon loses sight of it all, but he waits patiently while the months become decades. Eagerly he scans the approaches to the Father's House, joyfully anticipating the sight of Jesus again. Then, finally, after thirty-three years of faithful vigilance, Gabriel meets Jesus returning through the celestial pillars. He is horrified as he greets Christ: "Lord, what happened to you down there? Whence came these scars? What fiend would so mistreat the Father's Son? And the world you went to save? Did you save it, Lord?"

Then Jesus speaks, "No, Gabriel, I did not save humanity. I saved only a few and I saved them by these scars."

"But, Lord," protests the archangel, "what about the rest of humanity? Will they never be redeemed?"

"Gabriel, if the rest are ever saved, they will all be saved by these same wounds—there is no other way!"

✠ ✠ ✠

So, one by one, the cross cements the certainty of each of the things Christ claimed. The sun went dark to prove he was God's Son, as he had taught. Wooden beams and human anguish demonstrated the depths of God's love for his world. And, of course, all of it was to say that there is only one way to God. The cross saves even as it answers our grief.

There is one claim the cross would yet make—ourselves! The total us, mind you! The sum of all of our possessions, energies, and talents. From the very midst of our tears, we still see that Christ is God's Son. He has the right to possess our lives.

*M*an's mind cannot
grasp
the causes of events
in their completeness,
but the desire to find
those causes is implanted
in man's soul.

Leo Tolstoy
War and Peace

The Community of the Cross

God's Kingdom and Community

ut when they came to Jesus and found that he was already dead, they did not break his legs. Instead, one of the soldiers pierced Jesus' side with a spear, bringing a sudden flow of blood and water. The man who saw it has given testimony, and his testimony is true. He knows that he tells the truth, and he testifies so that you also may believe. These things happened so that the scripture would be fulfilled: "Not one of his bones will be broken" (John 19:33–36 NIV).

We who believe are the community of the cross. Here, in this community, the previously desperate and the previously lost come together and rehearse the glory of the kingdom community. We love the hymns, the sermons—

even the bad ones—because we remember that we once were lost but now belong to the society of the reclaimed. The people of need are now the people of grace.

Our current world is filled with many communities of need. "Hello, I'm Joe, I'm an alcoholic." So run the familiar words of greeting in the growing family of the chemically dependent. The local A. A. meetings are somewhat like the church. For in both communities the once-hopeless meet, confess their identity, speak of their need, and promise each other support. No wonder D. T. Niles defined the kingdom community as one beggar telling another where to get bread.

How fortunate are we to belong to a group that cares for us and, at the same time, demands care from us. In our culture so many men and women these days arrive home at night and are swallowed whole by electric garage doors to live utterly alone with few friends and little support. Their cries ring out for a community of people whom they need, and who need them.

The community of the cross is a fellowship of poverty. Years ago Louis Evely called the true church the "fraternity of the poor." He based this on Jesus' Beatitude: "Blessed are the poor in spirit" (Matt. 5:3). Only the poor are aware of their needs and let those needs draw them together in true community. We who call him "Lord" came to him because we knew we were destitute and hopeless and in great need. Our emptiness begged his completion and we were gloriously enfranchised.

We who love him found our finest friends in an hour of desperation, for there is a fellowship in suffering (Phil. 3:10). It is odd that while the Bible takes no pains to name the two bandits that died with Christ, tradition strongly names one of them as Dismus. Why do we need his name? Or why have we invented it? Because men should not suffer death together without knowing each other's names.

How much the word *cross* builds its community in our midst. Look at the countless ways we refer to the cross-bearing community. "If you don't bear the cross, then you can't wear the crown." "We are crucified with Christ." Even words like "cruciform" and "excruciating" (out of the cross), and "crucible" come from the Latin word for cross. As a symbol, the cross dominates our culture.

But, as a community member, I am fascinated by the primary models of John and Mary, the believing centurion, and the seeking thief. They are the only possible friends mentioned, along with Nicodemus who begged his body, as being with Christ at the moment of his death. Of these five, it is only John who might have endangered his life by being present. When Jesus begins to call his disciples, he is calling them to a legion of contempt. "Blessed are you when men shall persecute you," he said (Matt. 5:10). But he also said, "If you don't take up the cross, you cannot follow me" (Luke 9:23). If we link these two Scriptures together, it is easy to read him as saying, "Blessed is he who sits in the company of the crucified ones."

✠   ✠   ✠

What is the purpose of this company that the cross forges? Does the cross call them to exist to be only an accountability and support team to help each other through life? Hardly. The community of the cross is called to press the great saving dream of God upon the unredeemed world. It is not the will of the Father that any should perish (2 Peter 3:9). We know that Christ wants to draw all men to his Father that they might be saved

(John 6:37). His last instructions to the community were "Go into all the world and preach the gospel to every creature" (Matt. 28:19–20).

The community of the cross is not a society that exists primarily for its members (to bring support and require accountability). Rather, the community of the cross exists to serve its Master in the task of reclaiming all that Adam lost in the fall. We are there to bind up the broken and preach deliverance to the captives (Luke 4:18–19), which Jesus said was the reason that he had come. Now the reason to "be" is the reason that he came. His community exists to continue his work.

If God so loved the world that he gave his Son, the community is called to the task of living in the world and giving its own life to save this planet—which is the passion of God and must be the chief passion of the community of the cross. Our fellowship is only authentic when it is gathered around our saving task. Let us never talk to each other about how sweet is our fellowship with God until we admit that our fellowship exists to save the lost.

ᛉ   ᛉ   ᛉ

Each time I go to a church party and hear anyone brag about how "good" the fellowship is, I cringe. Fellowship is not a party. *Koinonia* as fellowship in the biblical sense is a word first used in Luke 5:10 to describe the fishermen apostles as business partners. Our *koinonia* means we are a community business: partners in the glorious calling of reaching out to reclaim God's world.

A. W. Tozer used to speak of both front-line and rear-guard *koinonia* fellowship. Rear-guard fellowship is Christian fellowship that majors on sociability. Frankly, we all like the rear guard best, for at the rear of the army the battle sounds are faint and far away. The generals and joint chiefs, our favorite friends, are all at the back of the army. Here with the most elite we feel best about ourselves. Here we may have tea and biscuits, secure in the knowledge that we are in no real danger. Here we are safe armchair soldiers who know friendship and laughter. But this is always more hollow than fellowship with the infantry at the front lines. There the roar of shell and shrapnel and the stabbing of hateful bayonets make life so precarious that those soldiers must defend each other at every parry, lest through their unguarded negligence a brother is killed. Those on the front line do not have leisurely rear-guard companionship. Nor is their laughter frequent. But they do live in the trenches, depending upon each other's vigilance to survive. These become what Elton Trueblood in another context called the company of the committed. They are what I am calling in this chapter the community of the cross. Those who claim a common task also need and defend each other. This must be our community's mission.

✠   ✠   ✠

Our community knows no self-sufficient members. We owe not only our peace of mind to the community, but indeed our entire existence. Self-sufficiency and cross-bearing do not go together in our "great fraternity of the poor." Those among us in this fraternity are often financially destitute, but when Jesus said, "Blessed are the poor in spirit" (Matt. 5:3), he was blessing those who have so little of the world's goods and are so emotionally in common need that we can never claim to be self-sufficient. Our neediness then causes us to reach out to others. During the earthquake in Guatemala some years ago, Howard Hughes, one of the wealthiest men in the West, was in the city hardest hit. When the destruction of the quake began to occur, Hughes climbed into a private helicopter and left. His wealth permitted that. But the poor Christians of Guatemala found a kind of wealth Hughes could never know. They needed each other, and community was born in their destitution.

So often I have knelt with my prayer group when my heart was breaking. In my thorn-in-the-flesh condition, I find that God's strength is made perfect in my weakness (2 Cor. 12:7–10), as my community of friends pray for me and give me the gift of their spirit. Then I discover why James says, "Confess your faults one to another and pray for one another that you may be healed" (James 5:16). We are the community of the cross: we reach within our need.

Can this be why Dismus the thief begs, "Lord, remember me when you come into your kingdom" (Luke 23:42)? Alone and dying, his aching shame begs anyone to see him and reach out. All those of us who share the crucified life, the dying life, are so very needy. So often I have attended a brother or sister who lay dying, and I have reached out to them. Always I find that their lives under judgment reach back. Crosses draw us toward each other as a company of needy souls.

☩   ☩   ☩

Let us examine those specific elements of the community that draw us to each other. First, there is *pain*. Not much needs to be said specifically about pain at this point, because it will be the theme of chapter 9. But at least let us acknowledge that when we hurt we reach out. Further, one of the strongest of all bonds of identity exists among those who have walked the same vale of suffering, who have endured an equal immensity of pain. I recently led a seminar in which two wheelchair paraplegics rolled into the classroom. They were having a wonderful time—never have I seen two souls who more understood and enjoyed each other's presence. But underneath the richness of their camaraderie, I saw the cross that each of them had encountered and were each day transcending. Pain makes brothers of all sorts of crucified souls.

✠ ✠ ✠

Another very potent element of the cross community is *shame*. Nakedness spawns an elegance of fellowship unattainable elsewhere. I used to see the films of Auschwitz and weep for those Jews who by the thousands had all their clothing stripped away. Solzhenitsyn says there is no more fearful experience than to have all your clothing stripped away and then be forced into an inter-rogation. It is not possible to answer as fully human when the trappings of our dignity are forcibly removed and we are less than persons in our own eyes.

It is Jesus who, naked on his cross, provides for us the only response to maintaining our self-esteem in the jaws of shame. One might argue that some crosses are of our own making, but the pain and the need are equally real. Yet the key thing about our community is that none join the enemy in mocking us at any hour of need. Shame is the chill that makes us throw a coverlet around our brother's nakedness, for we ourselves have been forgiven, and we will be forgiven as we lead the crucified life.

Shame is the great unanswerable reduction. We are caught! We are all pronounced "guilty" or "reviled" or "despised" and we cannot answer. But, on the back side of our shame, our humanity becomes accessible to us who were formerly arrogant. I once knew a woman who was unpleasantly "superior" to all those around her. She was avoided—often feeling hurt—because most people could not tolerate her arrogance. Then she was convicted of a crime and arraigned in court and became the butt of public scandal. Suddenly she was in need, and she did not merely reach for acceptance, she pleaded for it. Of course, she received acceptance, for her need was our object of touching concern. She saw how her self-sufficiency was a hollow sham and gladly became part of the community of the cross.

Paul cried out that Christ's shame is our glory, or that we glory in his shame. Here I personally love the crucified God the most. For in his almighty love he identified with us at the deepest level of degradation. Isaiah prophesied that he would be "despised and rejected of men" (Isa. 53:3), and yet he became the glorious center of our community. There is no level of earthly embarrassment we could endure that our Immanuel God has not already suffered. Have we known love like this? I come again to Christ the *archegos*—our pioneer and first-goer. He went first into the vale of shame; whatever we must undergo, he was there first.

I remember once how, through no fault of his own, a friend was forced into police court and his name appeared in the paper. He felt so ashamed that he was embarrassing the church. Then one woman in our community told him about a similar period in her life. Her family was smeared by the press and every morning had their pictures in the paper. "Your shame will pass," she said, "and when it does your brothers and sisters will be right here. That's what it means to be a Christian." Thank God for the acceptance of the glorious community of the cross.

✠   ✠   ✠

Finally, the community of the cross will always deal with our *aloneness*. "Strike the shepherd and the sheep will be scattered," said the Lord (Zech. 13:7). At the cross,

Jesus finds his friends evaporate into a mist of self-protection. Treachery and betrayal are cruel actions that each of us will feel at one time or another when standing or dying alone. There is also a real sense in which all of us feel an unseen threshold of loneliness. Even at a party in which we are most convivial, we often feel alone. The inmost part of ourselves is always separate and hidden. We are a part of what David Riesman called a "lonely crowd."

Dying alone, however, is the real pain of Calvary. Dying alone is immensely harder than living alone. In every case when I have been counselor to someone who has had a spouse die suddenly while he or she was away on some errand, much of the weeping was for the loneliness of the mate's dying. One of our hymns weeps, "Wounded and bleeding, for sinners pleading—Blind and unheeding—dying for me!"[1] "Promise you'll be there when I am dying," an elderly man begged me. Who can promise this? Yet I *could* promise that God in Christ, by example of Calvary, never let anyone die alone. Further, it is the assumption by all members of the community that we who belong will not tolerate loneliness for anyone if we can help it.

✝   ✝   ✝

We know that the cross is both our glory and our shame. Our power and our weakness. As we learn of it, we can never again consider it as matter-of-factly as we would the Dow-Jones average. And we have now established that it is not enough to see the cross only as history or theology. The cross is not merely the outcome of human events! Still, if it is not caused by man, it is the effect of human lawlessness. And it is both the hope and the fault of all who are part of the human race.

73

This cross was not made altogether with rough lumber, but hewn and mortised with our own indifference and insensitivity. There was a cross because Pilate was annoyed with Jesus rather than impressed with him. We are often annoyed by the infringement of God's agenda into our lives. There was a cross because Herod sought political favor. How often do our political candidates remind us of their born-again status? It's good for business on election day. There was a cross because the priests would not permit their spiritual sovereignty to be given over to Jesus. As a pastor, I sometimes want to be boss far too much to give Christ the freedom he needs to direct life in the church.

The sin of our authoritarian drives is sin against the community. To want power over those whom Christ has set free is a sin against the cross. Each of us should set our souls free from this avarice.

☩ ☩ ☩

There was a cross because there was a trial. The city of Jerusalem was host to this unfeeling court of judgments. However, shouts of violence have more than once run through the plaster canyons of the Holy City. The uncontrolled violence that produced Christ's execution has been the plight of her unhappy history. It was in this same Jerusalem in April 1961 that a thin, gray man, under armed surveillance, walked daily to a cage of bullet-proof glass and slipped on a headpiece that made it possible for him to communicate with a courtroom outside the transparent enclosure. A battery of more than five hundred reporters listened intently to the proceedings of the trial of Adolf Eichmann. There was much speculation about this more recent trial.

But Jesus' trial in Jerusalem, probably in April of A.D. 27, was a far more significant trial than Adolf Eichmann's. Long after the little Nazi-German who met justice in the Israeli court has been forgotten, the trial of A.D. 27 will be remembered. Here Pilate the judge and Jesus the defendant faced a sea of torches from which the warm scent of flaming pitch pervaded the brisk night air. Light from the flickering torches cast amber shadows over angry faces. We know our faces are there also. Here and there among the crowd one could see a face crowned by a phylactery, but light was at such a premium that one could not see the broad borders of their garments, which by day pronounced them "men of God." This, I suppose, was the jury! Are we not here, too?

Dwarfed by the majestic facade of the Fortress Antonia, Jesus and Pilate confronted each other. We, the would-be innocent, behold their confrontation. They represented two kingdoms, and the political kingdom has always appeared to be the dominant one. But as empires have come and gone, the real kingdom remains unchanged—this kingdom is in every generation the community of the cross. Now we cry inwardly, for we understand both kingdoms. We have been a part of both; we still are. One sends forth soldiers, the other evangelists. One divides the world into provinces, the other into mission fields. One proclaims the state, the other heralds the gospel of the Word.

Both kingdoms on the night of the trial were real, but Pilate could not understand the reality of Jesus' kingdom, as is obvious from the conversation of these two men, recorded in the Gospel of John. What was this folly that spoke of "the kingdom of the heart"? Hearts were "blood pumps" to Pilate, and many hearts had been forever silenced by Roman swords. What nonsense spoke of "the kingdom of God" within the empire of Caesar? Caesar fought with armor and blade, not with the sermons of a Nazarene carpenter or his disciples. Whatever Jesus' kingdom was, it clearly was no threat to Pilate's empire.

It is skepticism of this kind that makes crosses. But we can't push all the cross-makers back to the era of bronze helmets and parchment scrolls. Skepticism makes crosses for today's lonely minority students who brave classrooms filled with hatred in the name of fair play. Every time we see a cross you may be sure that *doubt* has given it cause. Our doubt ever wars against the community of faith. The chronic skeptic is in an ugly business. He or she tries to steal the confidence that individual members of the community extend to each other. It is too presumptuous to say that Pilate's skepticism was chronic. Still, it is correct to say that even if this doubt was the only one he ever had, it cost far too dearly. How different the whole episode might have ended if Jesus' claim to kingship had been met with respect rather than skepticism.

When we ignore Christ in our business lives, we say clearly that he is not King. A certain rancher of my acquaintance has large sections of wheat fields, extensive herds, and the best of grassland. Here and there his ranch is dotted by massive cylindrical oil tanks filled with the "black gold" from his wells. We are good friends, and often he has driven me through his numberless acres of land. It is his empire. He is a member of the kingdom of God. But somehow I have felt that there is no room for the community of the cross within his empire.

My friend's attitude and aspirations could be duplicated, most likely, in every other occupation and profession. We live in the age of the private "kingdom builder"!

We dream of finances and security, of homes and cars, of retirement and comfort. These petty grievances are all part of our little empires. Nothing wrecks the goals of God's community like the driving privatization of ambition. Our appetites for the material are only a small function of our micro-empires. So many among us are monarchs in miniature and, like Pilate, we question Jesus' right to kingship.

But Christ's wholeness transcends our needy souls. There was something in Jesus that could genuinely claim kingship. We are all illegitimate kings, bogus monarchs. Jesus' kingdom would have claimed even Pilate as a subject had he been willing. And it can claim us as subjects, too.

We are all too willing to concede that Jesus is the King of the Jews. We are even willing to concede that Jesus is the King of most Gentiles. But when it comes to our own petty microcosms of existence, *we* are kings and not Jesus. Further, we often shrug off the community of God and its redeeming work in his world. What a heartbreak to realize that some of us, like Pilate of old, never know the joy of owning Jesus Christ as King of kings. Oh, the cost of Pilate's doubt!

✳ ✳ ✳

Pilate did not consider Jesus either king or a threat to Rome. He released Jesus into the custody of Herod, who seemed to possess a Roman privilege that allowed him to judge but not to convict.

Herod is a man of whom Luke says, "He desired to see a sign." Poor Herod! Did he not know that this same Jesus had refused to leap from the pinnacle of the temple merely to proclaim himself Messiah? Jesus never profaned the power of God by performing signs and miracles for self-aggrandizement. But those in the community of the cross are satisfied with God's presence in their midst. They have no need of a sign. They want to know he lives within the community, but because they are willing to trust that his presence is with them, they do not demand that he make himself known in some miracle.

Herod sought a spectacular something. He loved spectacle! The Jews were always speaking of divided seas, flaming serpents, and fiery furnaces. Herod would have liked to have seen some such sign (Luke 23:8). Nevertheless, Jesus was certainly not the one to gratify any of Herod's inordinate desires for spectacle.

Herod is legion in the churches of our day. Fields of suburbanite Christians migrate from congregation to congregation, propelled by a wanderlust for the greatest Christian show on earth. This ecclesiastical restlessness keeps the holy work of God's saving community at sea. Its saving work cannot prosper while the community wanders in search of something glitzy to fill its shallow heart. Where the reverbs and colored spots meet is only a place of plastic discipleship, where the lost sheep demonstrate how lost they are by begging the shepherd to replace his crook of pastoral care with a vaudeville hat and cane.

$$\text{╬} \quad \text{╬} \quad \text{╬}$$

If Pilate teaches us doubt and vacillation, Herod teaches us to desire a spectacular sign. This damnable desire for dramatics has duped us—even drugged us—with a narcotic lure to the theatrical rather than the submissive. To King Herod, Jesus did not seem to have enough of the charismatic power that a reformer and Messiah should possess. Jesus must have seemed foolish and small-time to Herod, for after thirty-six recorded miracles,

Jesus refused to perform even one small sign for his own interests.

Jesus is no magician who wants to mystify us by pulling rabbits out of hats. He is not a trickster. He came not to entertain us but to redeem us. Jesus did not come to offer us a spotlight and gold slippers, he came to offer us the right to die in his defense and for his Good News.

✠ ✠ ✠

In principle there are many Pilates among us who deny Jesus' right to be King; there are also many Herods in our midst who seek a sign. We of the Space Age are indeed lovers of spectacle. It has become our reverence, even in the realm of religion. We clamor for display. We cry for natural evidences of the supernatural and physical evidences of the metaphysical.

There are those who seem to feel that there is no salvation but a spectacular one. Have we not heard them say, "I'll tell you, people just aren't saved like they used to be"? Why do they say this? Are not people still saved by repentance and faith? "Yes," they continue, "but now people don't weep when they are saved." It is indeed a blessing to any Christian to see someone so overwhelmed by the magnanimity of God's redemption that he or she cannot restrain tears. Yet it must be realized that this person's salvation is no more extensive than the salvation of one who comes to Christ with a demeanor that is placid and thoughtful. We are often reluctant to admit that salvation without an emotional display is possible. In some respects we are little different from those of the first century who said, "Lord, show us a sign."

Herod, blinded by his administrative world, could not see that supernatural signs would have completely eliminated the necessity for faith. His sin is also ours. For that which we can see plainly, we need no faith. Faith comes because there are some realities that we do not apprehend with the five senses. God does not often speak to us through thunderous signs that shatter the air. More often he speaks in whispers barely audible to our inmost heart.

Herod missed the kingdom because of his wooden insensitivity. Let us beware such surface sins. It is not frequently that God sets aside the laws of nature and speaks in some miraculous, supernatural way. There have been few Constantines who saw letters of flame in the sky. Yet there have been many Wesleys who have felt those imperceptible flames of faith strangely warm their hearts. Let us cry out to have Wesley's Christ rather than Herod's empty desire for display.

✛　✛　✛

Yet we do hunger for God's direction in life. Because of that yearning, some seminary students may be struggling with all that is in them. Does the Lord want them to serve in their home state or across the sea? How easy it would be if the Lord gave them a clear signal: one ball of fire for this land and two balls of fire if he wished them to serve elsewhere—a "one if by land and two if by sea" sort of beacon. But, as Jesus said to the sign-mongering apostles who were unable to heal a demoniac, there are certain things that come only by prayer and fasting. This is the way the prophets and apostles found the will of God, and this is how we find it.

The cross of Christ has triumphed. In its own subtle, silent force in the world, it has claimed us. It never seeks to call attention to itself. It despises the kind of clamor and display that produced it. It reaches to us to teach us the emptiness of our show-biz discipleship.

Do we not then show ourselves to be a little spiritually lazy when we seek a spectacular evidence of God or of his will? We, the saving community, talk earnestly to God and have no need of signs. The wheel that rolled for Ezekiel by the river Chebar need not roll for us; we can pray—we the many—as one. We are free to be a community of prayer, bringing our own inwardness into encounter against all secular shallowness, even that which has camped out in the church.

We would be much better off if we said to Jesus not, "Lord, show us a sign," but, "Lord, teach us to pray!" Let no man accuse us of being Herods. Let us not be found in the ranks of those whose only God is spectacle and whose only benediction is "Lord, show us a sign!"

✠   ✠   ✠

Pilate and Herod may have precipitated the cross event, but there were those present who would have prevented it if they could have done so. These were they who believed Jesus. Belief is the antidote to Pilate's doubt and Herod's empty spirit of display. Faith caused them to follow the Teacher. Their following left us an example of that which vindicates the cause of the cross.

In Luke 23:55 there is a mention of the women who had followed Christ all the way from Galilee. How important it is for Jesus to have followers! Christianity only exists as long as Jesus has followers; when there are no followers, there is no kingdom community. The late Charles Malik, outstanding Lebanese statesman, implied that communism is advancing because there are too few followers of Jesus. A past president of the General Assembly of the United Nations (1958), he said the Christendom can be preserved only if we return to Christ and follow him:

In Christianity, God became man: think of the great honor to us weak men! Indeed, if you ask yourself honestly what it is that you wish to preserve in "our way of life," you will find that the things you value most are based squarely on the bedrock of religion. Honor. Duty. Justice. Freedom. Tolerance. Charity. Sharing. Repentance. These are also Christian concepts. Does it not follow, then, that if we are to preserve them, we must return to Christ as our Lord and Savior, and therefore as the guide for everyday living?[2]

If Christianity is to be preserved, we must follow Jesus. He must ever stand at the center of our community.

It is in *following* that our Christianity becomes vital for individuals within the community. Groups do not follow Christ; individuals follow Christ. It is not "they" or "we" who follow, but "I." The kingdom of God is never a pluralized call. We each embrace it alone or not at all. It is said that the Galileans followed, but they followed individually. Regardless of what the rest of the community does, each of us must singularly follow Christ. We need to adopt for ourselves the resolution of Jonathan Edwards:

Resolved: that every man should live to the glory of God. Resolved Second: That whether others do this or not, I will.[3]

With this endeavor let us follow Christ, exactly as did the Galilean women in Luke 23. They are the real heroines of that chapter. They do not question Jesus' right to be King! They are not bound to him because they seek a sign! They follow him because of love. All they hold in life is bound up in this man Jesus. When he breathed out his last on Golgotha, something vital in their breasts shriveled into nonexistence. Yet they are our teachers.

These women had followed from Galilee. It is such a long way from Galilee to Calvary. Maybe not in miles or furlongs or kilometers, but it is a long way. Between Galilee and Calvary there were tears, humiliation, heartbreak, and "the thousand natural shocks that flesh is heir to."[4] Somewhere between the two, the kingdom of God splintered and fragmented into little groups of fearful believers. For those who followed, God died between Galilee and Calvary. But they followed! Who were these women? They were part of that small but newborn growing community of the cross.

✠　✠　✠

What a tribute is paid to those Galileans who followed! Judas betrayed, but they followed! Peter denied, but they followed! Pilate questioned, but they followed! Even when all hope was gone, they followed to the very door of the tomb. Remarkable? Hardly! Let us not compliment them, for that is what the community is supposed to be. That's just normal "kingdom Christianity." It's just that we have been myopic for so long that we have begun to see the normal as abnormal. If they could follow Jesus in the face of such crushing despair, should not we—who know the hope of the resurrection—follow?

Jesus was a king! He died under a trilingual sign that proclaimed him *Rex, Basileus, Melek*—King! Let us own him as King and follow him, not as sign-mongers, but as subjects in need, accountable to each other in the community of the King!

*M*any follow Jesus
to the breaking of bread,
but few to the drinking
of the chalice
of his Passion

Thomas à Kempis
The Imitation of Christ

5

The Tree of Treachery

When We Are Traitors—
When We Are Betrayed

esus answered, "It is the one to whom I will give this piece of bread when I have dipped it in the dish." Then, dipping the piece of bread, he gave it to Judas Iscariot, son of Simon. As soon as Judas took the bread, Satan entered into him (John 13:26–27 NIV).

Now Judas, who betrayed him, knew the place, because Jesus had often met there with his disciples (John 18:2 NIV).

"*Et tu, Brute!*" are the famous plaintive words of Julius Caesar to Brutus as Brutus stabbed him. Who are the arch traitors in history and literature? For Othello, it is

Iago; for Washington, Benedict Arnold; for Jesus, it is Judas. We, like these others who were betrayed, are ever surprised by the traitors who smile at us with offerings of friendship while they fondle concealed daggers to undo us. "How could you do this to me?" we cry in disappointment. We may protect ourselves by putting on an air of diffidence, but we are never quite the same again.

╬ ╬ ╬

The cross is at least on a surface level the result of one man's treachery. But in Judas we see at least one other face, the face of some false lover or betraying confidant. Nathaniel Hawthorne's *Young Goodman Brown* comes on a "black mass" in a New England wood one hapless night. As he passes, he sees the most revered Christians of the parish dancing naked in demonic ritual. He is not only shattered at that moment, but for the rest of his life his whole view of anyone he meets is cankered by what he doesn't know about people.

It is the nature of sinful humanity that we are all traitors, and yet we despise treachery. Intolerant of the Judas syndrome in others, we are blind to it in ourselves. In all honesty, treachery is probably the foundational transgression upon which all other sin is built. Is not the original sin Adam and Eve's hiding in their treachery with half-eaten fruit, hiding in vain from him whom they have betrayed?

Each time I commit a willful sin, it is as though I have knowingly betrayed obedience by my self-will. But, in the strictest sense, only close friends can commit treachery. Those we barely know may lie. Political leaders may be tyrants and behave treasonously, but only a close friend can act treacherously.

✠   ✠   ✠

Forgiving treachery may be duck soup for our grace-rich God, but it is likely the most difficult sin we are ever asked to forgive. I remember a poor woman who found out her husband had been regularly committing adultery with his secretary. "He has betrayed me," she cried. "I will never, ever forgive him!"

A doctor of my acquaintance told me about his ruggedly handsome son, who left his seminary training for the ministry and entered into the gay community in Seattle. As if this was not heartbreaking enough, this son "fell in love and became engaged to another athlete." These successful young businessmen openly announced their homosexual relationship and exchanged engagement rings. Their affair was ultimately consummated in engraved invitations and a very fashionable wedding, complete with cake and champagne. My doctor friend was at first shattered, but later consumed with hostility over what he called his son's "betrayal."

✠   ✠   ✠

Well, how is the cross to answer these issues of betrayal? First of all, the treachery did not surprise our Lord. He knew it was coming, and he set Judas free to do it. If we remember that Judas seems predestined for the job (he had "a devil" from the beginning [John 6:70]), it is still to Jesus' great credit that he did not ask the disciples physically to coerce Judas into loyalty.

While we can never know who is the potential traitor in our lives, we must forever be setting our friends free from the necessity of being loyal. Only when we set them free can we be sure that their loyalty is spontaneous and uncoerced. Only then will their love be meaningful. Since Jesus expected treachery, he could live realistically. I do not advocate that we should be negative or live under some glowing cloud of our own fashioning. I just think that human nature ought to be understood and that we ought never to gush in astonishment at anyone's behavior. All of us are capable of willfully acting in such strong self-interest that it must be interpreted as treachery by someone who trusts us.

But the outstanding thing that the cross teaches us is that it exists to forgive all sin, treachery included. If Judas hangs himself and perishes eternally, it is not because the cross lacked the power to forgive him. It is that he never appropriated that forgiveness.

The cross is the capital place for magnanimity. Jesus was caught up in a project so huge that he would not distract himself with petty resentments. We do not hear him whimper that Judas had done him dirty. Rather, he forges on with God's redeeming plan for his life. What excellence and wisdom there is in this!

✚   ✚   ✚

To find God's plan for our lives is to crucify ourselves to all sniveling need to find encouragement, or even to seek counsel, when someone has injured us. When I remember that many without Christ are dependent on my faithfulness, I can sail through times of discouragement and betrayal without having to distract myself with self-pity.

How do I do this?

I believe there are two factors that bestow this spirit of largesse. First, there is the direct example of Jesus, which inspires my need to be like him—to act like him in the crisis. Needless to say, I live through difficulties in a positive manner when my emulation of Jesus derives directly from my continual conversation with him. In other words, I overcome treachery by talking and listening to Christ. Actually, it is not so much that I overcome it; I am so preoccupied with Jesus that I fail to notice it.

A second factor that contributes to this largesse is the indwelling Spirit of Christ. How so? Let us remember that the Spirit is interested in my submission to Jesus. Nearly all our littleness of being comes from direct egotism. When we whimper, we are by our evident mood serving our need to be stroked.

Often (but not often enough), I have felt the overwhelming presence of the Spirit draw me to a rapt hush. This state always focuses on the beauty and dignity of Christ. At such moments my resentment of others becomes impossible, for resentment itself finds no way to struggle to mind when the relationship is at its compelling zenith.

Thus always is all our treachery resolved.

✠   ✠   ✠

Let us examine the actual events of that first Maundy Thursday to see exactly how it was that Jesus modeled the overcoming life. That Thursday came as it always had. Nothing was different about it. A young rabbi, followed by a dozen husky men, sat down at a massive table, and a flagon of wine was emptied into a single cup. Each of the men had anticipated Thursday's party as a time of levity and warmth, but when the hour had come there was an unspoken dread in the air that choked lightheartedness. It seemed to be such an ordinary Thursday and, beyond it, only an ordinary Friday. But nothing was ordinary. A ghastly picture of Friday lay unseen on the surface of Thursday's wine. Ominously the portent floated on the deep-red liquid, framed by the oval rim of the metal chalice. What was the omen that lay unnoticed on the crimson-purple surface of the wine? It was the picture of a man with a hammer, who talked to himself as if he were lonely and unused to such Fridays as this. Many years ago I wrote in my journal how Christ spoke in soundless words from the surface of the cup:

On with Friday's grisly business!
Let the broad arm raise the sledge!
Let the hammer ring out upon the nails.
I must not flinch when the crimson flows—
He's only a carpenter—a craftsman who claimed too
   much.
"I need a black nail, soldier."
Give me your hand, carpenter. What a strange man you
   are!
You stretch forth your hand too eagerly—too willingly, as
   though I was going to shake it, not nail it to a tree.
Steady, man. The first stroke of the hammer is easiest for
   me and hardest for you.
For me the first blow meets only the resistance of soft
   flesh.
The hardwood beneath drives much slower.
For you the first blow is the worse.
It brings the ripping pain and the bright gore.
The wood beneath your wrist does not feel and bleed as
   you do.

Suddenly one of the Twelve must have jolted the table, and the ripples in the wine erased the unseen specter. Then that yet-unpierced hand reached for the cup. Thus our Christ began his dying work and our saving work on that Thursday. We needed life, and so he lifted the cup. We might argue long whether Jesus died on Thursday or on Friday. Of course, Friday was the day they raised up the cross, but Thursday was the day he faced it in Gethsemane.

I suspect that Thursday was the day he lived between ourselves and his Father. To please his Father was to sacrifice himself for us. He knew his dying would be made possible by his one desire to please his Father. And so who can deny that his dying was in Gethsemane, when he said, "Yes, Father"? In that resolve his life was already on the cross for our sake, although the actual bleeding would come later. Jesus had us in mind when he lifted the cup. He passed it to a dozen men with Aramaic names, but make no mistake about it, he drank a cup of ages and historical sequence. He thought of us even as he gave the cup to those at hand.

While he drank, Christ had no misgivings about the morrow. He knew that somewhere in the city lay his cross, already hewn. Furthermore, he knew that one of his disciples was a turncoat who that very Thursday had been haggling betrayal with graybeards in the temple. The die was cast. At this same hour on Friday he would be sealed in Joseph's mausoleum. In a few hours that Thursday would be forever gone, and Jesus would be facing an ordeal that few men ever faced: the Roman cross. He was tired, worn with the dread of it all, and needed rest for the brutal Friday. Still, there had to be one final attempt to explain to the disciples the essence of redemption.

As he lifted the cup he said to them, "This do in remembrance of me!" (1 Cor. 11:24). In effect, he was saying, "Remember tomorrow! For what shall happen tomorrow concerns everyone who ever shall live. God shall have nails in his hands tomorrow. God shall be scourged and mocked tomorrow. Tomorrow, I shall die. Remember tomorrow."

The Latin base word for *communion* (to be one with) describes both our need and his intention. Our Savior, not yet wounded in his hands, drinks and passes the wine to us. We drink in our oneness together, and all the world who will believe is made our brothers and sisters in his cup.

Dramatically Jesus had reached for Thursday's loaf. With almost sudden violence, he tore it in two and said what seemed to say, "Do you see this bread? Eat it! Tomorrow my body will be torn like this!" Then he breathed a prayer and lifted the cup and spoke the phrase whose larger meaning was: "My blood will flow as easily as this wine. Drink it and remember tomorrow!"

One by one the men considered his chilling prophecies of the yet-unborn Friday. Silently the cup rose to the lips of a publican. Then a fisherman received the cup and drank of it and passed it to a zealot. Their eyes, glistening with sorrow, were fastened on the Master. With his grim predictions still in the air, each man drank and passed the cup to the next.

⧎   ⧎   ⧎

Somehow Jesus' cup transcends that simple table and the room; indeed it transcends that time. The wine and the blood are ours. We are saved and in communion— "one with" our wondrous Lord in the dying and the living and the hope.

The contagion of the melancholy that had come over the Twelve kept conversation to a minimum as they left the upper room and hurried toward the park in the valley of the Kidron. Are we not there? Do we not rise—all ages—from that narrow table and once again join the millions of lovers who have lifted that sweet cup as members of his glorious, growing family? And so we walk through the purple shadows and gray buildings. And we, the saved of all ages, hear Jesus say:

> You will all fall from your faith; for it stands written: "I will strike the shepherd down and the sheep will be scattered."
> . . . Peter answered, "Everyone else may fall away, but I will not."
> Jesus said, "I tell you this: today, this very night, before the cock crows twice, you yourself will disown me three times."
> But he insisted and repeated: "Even if I must die with you, I will never disown you."
> And they all said the same (Mark 14:27–31 NEB).

This is the tragedy of Thursday: eleven men pledged themselves to commitments they would never fulfill. They were but the strong promises of weak men. We likewise make strong promises but are weak people. We need Christ simply because of our large professions and our little deeds.

⧊   ⧊   ⧊

So Thursday became known as the day of apostolic treason and betrayal. The baleful treachery of Judas is Thursday's tale. Judas, the Benedict Arnold of the apostolate, the arch-Brutus of the early church, was a knight of the new kingdom. In spite of Matthew's experience with facts and figures, Judas had been ordained the keeper of the purse. He was the steward of the combined legacies of thirteen men. He disbursed the funds and was doubtless conscientious in the spending of all that had been committed to his keeping.

It may well have been Judas' dedication to faithful accounting that led him to look with disfavor on the King and his kingdom. For three years, Jesus had been speaking of a great kingdom. Perhaps an impatient Judas scorned the fact that after all that time this "great kingdom" still numbered only twelve subjects. Even so, it was no small task to manage the scant economies of thirteen men. Feeding them alone was a strain on the budget that kept Judas scratching his head and calculating expenses. To trim unnecessary spending, the group often lived out-of-doors, sleeping in open parks and gardens like the one in which the apostles were sleeping on the night of Jesus' arrest. Typical of all good treasurers, Judas probably resented unneeded spending and extravagant waste of money.

⚓ ⚓ ⚓

This resentment of waste may have been the very issue behind Thursday's bargain with the priests. Only four days before in nearby Bethany, Mary, the sister of the resurrected Lazarus, had done something that appeared to Judas to be wasteful and extravagant sentiment (John 12:1–3). She had taken a pound of spikenard, a costly cosmetic, and poured it on Jesus' feet. Spikenard was a rare Himalayan flower, and many thousands of these precious blossoms had to be crushed to produce a pound of the fragrant oil. The ointment was so costly that the price of the one pound that Mary had lavished on Jesus would have kept some poor family in food for a whole year.

The price of the spikenard would have doubtless gone a long way also in supporting an itinerant rabbi and his retinue. Judas explosively condemned the waste: "Why was not this ointment sold for three hundred pence, and given to the poor?" (John 12:5 KJV). Nevertheless, Jesus defended Mary's deed and spoke with a curt finality that Judas could not possibly mistake: "Let her alone: against the day of my burying hath she kept this" (v. 7 KJV). It may have been that Judas felt a stinging repudiation in this, and his brooding, injured self-respect was the seedbed of Thursday's betrayal. Wounded pride often gives birth to vengeance. The littleness in the heart of the man from Kerioth may have wished some "get even" destruction on Jesus. But whatever the motive for betrayal may have been, Judas yielded to its hellish impulses and agreed to sell his Master into the hands of religious butchers, whose vengeance also burned against Christ.

⚜ ⚜ ⚜

Thirty pieces of silver was the contract price agreed on. It was a pitiful sum whose current equivalent would be twenty-four dollars. Can this be the very Judas who objected to wasteful spending? Judas, this is such poor economics. Twenty-four dollars for silencing lips that uttered the Sermon on the Mount! Twenty-four pitiful dollars for the fastening of hands that broke the bread of redemption in the upper room! There is none who can excuse your betrayal, Judas! You well deserve to be called Satan's Saint!

> God Slayer! Savior-Killer!
> Murderer of Mary's Son!
> Butcher-fiend of Love and Grace!
> Monster! Traitor! Evil One!
>
> It is you, who raised his cross,
> Stained his palms, and pierced his side.

Turncoat against the Son of God,
You had the Master crucified.

Whenever evil men loathe light,
And Hell seeks to include us,
Decent men will curse your name,
Darkened, Son of Satan, Judas!

Calvin Miller
Poems of Protest and Faith

There is an ugliness and loneliness in betrayal. It alienates the betrayer from the betrayed. So it was with Judas that Thursday night on the way to Gethsemane. He had bargained to lead the officials to the person of Jesus. Following Judas to the garden where Jesus was spending the night was a detachment of temple police. Even though the betrayer was in the company of soldiers, a new loneliness was stealing into his life. It was that utter loneliness that never again found a friend.

⚜ ⚜ ⚜

Judas walked with reluctance amidst the clanking of armor and the pungent odor of blazing pitch from a dozen torchfires. The soldiers' swords, which Judas was sure would not be needed, glistened in the starlight as the temple guard entered the garden. The sleeping, groggy apostles awoke, too stunned to run or fight, while Judas advanced to Jesus, kissed him, and said, "Hail, Master!" The kiss was the signal of identification, and Christ was arrested.

Here is the most bitter kiss of recorded time. It is history's greatest lie—the kiss that stood for nothing. Anyone who saw it might have reasoned, "My, how Judas loves the Master." The kiss seemed to say that, but the

presence of the soldiers said something else. Jesus had
nothing to fear from the soldiers and the priests, for they
were clearly his enemies, and declared enemies had never
intimidated him. It was Iscariot, his lover in pretense, who
alone was able to destroy him. The greatest enemies of
Christ have ever been those who play-act as his closest
friends. The cause of Christ has suffered little from its
alleged enemies. It is because of its pretended lovers that
the kingdom has been kept in splints and bandages for
the past two thousand years.

✠   ✠   ✠

Judas was the ancestor of all those in our generation
who wear the double mask of allegiance and treason. How
many millions of us in this century have "hailed the Master," then warped his honor by lying, cheating, or profan-
ing his name! Many who would scorn Judas' betrayal for
thirty pieces of silver betray Christ daily for less. How
often are we the pretended lovers of Christ who throng
today's churches and fall asleep in Gethsemane? The
Judas kiss has become so common that even sincere love
for Christ is often called suspect. In any present list of
disciples, the traitors might outnumber the true. Judas-
type treachery still makes many crosses in today's
churches. It fabricates them out of gossip and half-truths
and then hangs the reputations of good men on the
betrayals of the double-minded. Betrayal always tres-
passes love and confidence. We are saved but not loyal.
We say, "Lord, Lord," but do not the things that he says
(Luke 6:46).

As it was in the case of Judas and Jesus, so it always
is. A pastor of my acquaintance had given to his secretary his utter trust and confidence. She betrayed his trust.
Never openly, mind you, for a Judas never makes his bar-

gains in the sunlight. She did it by leaving question marks in her statements about her pastor, being sure that her every comment about him had some double meaning. Her telephone calls from the church office were full of innocent inflections that packed insinuations into the truth, which she always spoke. Her treachery so hacked at the pastor's respect that he left the church. This is the way the Judas sin always eats at love and trust. Yet the traitor forever appears a person of peace.

Betrayal inevitably ushers in that empty question about the worth and meaning of existence. We hate the Judas spirit only in others. We tolerate it in ourselves. And we are left lonely and disconsolate. If a man's greatest lover and confidant hucksters him off for profit, where does the man then look for meaning in a world filled with hypocrisy? Jesus could scarcely bear this beginning of rejection from one so dear. How he must grieve our faithless treachery! I believe that tears of disappointed love were swimming in his eyes as he voiced his heartache: "Judas, would you betray the Son of Man with a kiss?" (Luke 22:48). To those of us who harbor Judas in our hearts, he surely says, "Drive a dagger in my heart if you must, but don't preface it with pretense." We must not acquit ourselves by blaming Gethsemane on Judas. It is our current treachery that hurts the current Christ.

Shakespeare has his dying Caesar say to the conspirator who was his friend, "And you, Brutus!" In the same tender tone that did not want to believe Judas' treason, Jesus was saying, "And you, Judas!" From this point on, Judas searched for some meaning in life that would make living worthwhile.

Here, in such a quest for a reason to "be," our own betrayal always ends. Because, as traitors, we find so little worthwhile in our lives, we question the value of all life. By our fallen loyalty, we prove to ourselves that our love and confidence are undependable; then we suspect all love as having faults such as ours. Because we do so poorly with our trust, we may falsely come to the conclusion that there is no unfailing love, and hence no life has a reason to be lived. How foolish that we presume against the whole. Just because we are void of meaning does not mean that many are not hungry for a reason to believe.

✠　✠　✠

The Judas life does not always end in suicide, but it always ends empty and hungry. Beyond Gethsemane there was nothing left for Judas but a gnarled, twisted tree on a canyon rim. There, from a knotted limb, hung a heavy rope, and in the chafing noose of its braided hemp hung the head of faithless Judas. Who knows whether in that last moment of life, he breathed again the treacherous formula, "Hail, Master."

Do not feel that Judas died an unusual death. Our betrayal also contains the seeds of our own self-destruction. We may not kill ourselves with suicide, but we will kill our usefulness and our devotion. And while we may have breath and pulse, the true and uncreated life will still be missing. Somewhere on the back side of every cross is a hangman's tree. Each time we betray Christ we stab at our own existence. Anyone who betrays the Lord of Life had better beware. Hell is God's ash can for traitors. Be careful lest you sell all the meaning from your life for spangles and betray your Christ for silver.

Thursday was Judas Day! It stood for betrayal, but it also stood for broken commitment. We have already seen how Simon Peter, on the way to the garden, pledged to stand by Jesus, whatever might come. What magnificent promises he made. Oh, if only he had stood by those vows! "To prison and to death, but never to deny you," vowed Simon (Luke 22:33). So promised all the disciples.

⚓ ⚓ ⚓

Had the disciples lived their promises, there would have been twelve crosses silhouetted against the Judean sky that next day. Had they been the men they claimed to be on Thursday, Friday might have seen every one of them flogged and crowned with thorns. There could have been such blessed fellowship in their sufferings. They might have sung the rightness of their cause in a great chorus, from a dozen gallows. Together in death they might have linked nail-scarred hands and entered into glory—the faithful company of the crucified lovers of Christ.

In the prosperity of our times, one wonders how many disciples would die for Christ if called on. Would there be many crosses that would crowd poor Golgotha? It's only a guess, but I can only conjecture that when so many in contemporary Christianity live totally for themselves, they would not likely die for anyone else. Unless there were a couple of criminals to grace his modern hilltop once again, I suspect that Christ would die alone.

All the loyal promises of his twelve life-pledging friends went unfulfilled. The disciples vanished when the conflict came. They all fled, except for the youngest, John. How Christ must have leaned on that young man. He must have felt his silent strength in the judgment hall. He saw John's eyes study the stone floor when his clothing was stripped away. He loved the man whose cheeks glistened silver with tears when his Master was stretched to the whipping post. How much it must have meant to Jesus

100

to look down from Friday's stake and see John standing at his feet, recklessly and courageously declaring himself the friend of a blasphemer. None of the other disciples were there to so declare themselves.

☩ ☩ ☩

Just where were all the gallant men who declared their Thursday "Pledge of Allegiance" by dramatically slicing the air with great gestures of loyalty? One of them waited by the fire in the little courtyard before the judgment hall. Simon Peter was possessed of that half-devotion of so many modern disciples. He loved Jesus too much to utterly forsake him, but not enough to go all the way with him to judgment. He vacillated between leaving altogether and going on into the judgment hall with John. It is this unsteady devotion that Peter Marshall described in one of his prayers: "We are too Christian really to enjoy sinning, and too fond of sinning really to enjoy Christianity."[1] Simon Peter was neither an unswerving devotee nor an out-and-out deserter. In this neither-nor state of mind he waited in the courtyard.

The chill of the crisp night air may have prompted Peter to move closer to the fire, where others had gathered for warmth and conversation. The topic of conversation seemed to be the strange nocturnal proceedings of the trial then under way. Peter's mind ran feverishly over the fireside chatter, but his face registered little. The tongues of light that danced on glowing fagots in the courtyard fire suddenly brought Peter's face into full illumination so that a young woman in the group, with startling suddenness, lifted her finger toward Peter and said, "This man was also with him." Only the deep bronze tone of the old sailor's leathery complexion kept the hot blood from showing as it rushed to his face and he blurted out the denial, "Woman,

I know him not!" This treachery put its foot in the door of his heart and beckoned full-grown betrayal to enter.

Instinctively, Peter drew back a little from the direct light of the flames. He pulled his hood a little further forward on his forehead. Those titan hands, made strong by tugging soggy nets, trembled like the infirm fingers of an old person. But the shadows were not deep enough to hide him. A bystander, who perhaps had heard Jesus teach and was sure that Peter was with him, affirmed what the girl had said: "You are one of them." With a tinge of anger at the charge of being disciple to an accused blasphemer, Peter answered hotly, "Man, I am not!" (Luke 22:58 NIV).

The accusations subsided temporarily and Peter could have wished them over with. Time dragged on. Inside the hall, Christ was being victimized by cankered justice and false witnesses. Outside, Peter was the victim of his own shabby dedication and a trio of accusers. After an hour had passed, a third man, who had sat by the fireside and studied Peter's Galilean brogue, made an abrupt accusation: "Surely you are one of them, for your accent gives you away" (Matt. 26:73 NIV). A fit of temper seized the big apostle and in anger he swore and cursed his accusers and the stigma of discipleship of which they accused him.

Imagine this great hulk of a man gone out of control. One of his hands closes on the clothing of his accuser. The other hand clenches into a fist, which Simon Peter brandishes like a weapon in the air above the poor man's head as he shouts with white-hot profanity, "I know not the man!" Startled by his violence, all eyes in the little enclosure fall instantly on Peter. Shocked into dumbness, no one speaks. In that soundless moment, while Peter's fist trembles in unleashed anger, through the still night air comes the piercing scream of a cock. Its shrill cry, like the unsteady note of a trumpet, calls to mind Peter's Thursday promise. He releases his trembling accuser as tears come with stinging suddenness to his eyes. He buries his head in his huge hands and sobs his way out of the plaza. He has been unfaithful to his Lord. Thursday has meant nothing. Nothing that he promised has he done. His Lord would soon be on a cross, and his loneliness would be unspeakable because of Peter's treachery. Thursday, day of broken vows, is gone for Simon and the rest who promised all.

Once we have known the exhilaration of love committed unto Christ, we must guard ourselves lest there come to us some bitter Thursday of denial and betrayal. Somewhere in the process of undedicated living, by a thoughtless deed we may forget all we have affirmed. Is our commitment to the Master authentic? We must examine it. Try it. Prove it. We who have promised Christ all must go to the very cross that makes us so afraid. Only as we conquer our greatest fears can we measure the size of our commitment.

If you will be My disciple, deny yourself.

If you will possess the pleased life, despise this present life.

If you will be exalted in heaven, humble yourself in this world.

If you will reign with Me, bear the cross with Me.

Thomas à Kempis
The Imitation of Christ

6

Who Caused the Cross?

Answering Our Own Accountability

hen Pilate saw that he was get-ting nowhere, but that instead an uproar was starting, he took water and washed his hands in front of the crowd. "I am innocent of this man's blood," he said. "It is your responsibility!" (Matt. 27:24 NIV).

We did it! What? The cross—we did it! The debt, the crime, the need for it all is ours. Let's examine how it was when he died, how we became accountable. The questions we must answer are: "How was it that first Good Friday?" "Who caused the cross?"

Let us imagine the scenario that day. Perhaps there is an expression of terror on the face of the first bandit that day. With a sobriety born out of fear, he watches the soldiers make ready his torture, possessed of that muddled sort of reasoning that controls the mind of a convict who idly waits in death row. The condemned man's thoughts are abruptly interrupted when the soldiers come to fasten him to his death. He struggles against them. His leg lashes out and sends one of the soldiers sprawling into the dirt. His hands clench into fists and strike out at breasts protected by polished armor. He spits in their faces and curses them and the laws of their state. But soon his execution is underway, and he is securely fastened to the instrument of death. When the first pains rack his body, his thirst-crazed lips part and issue a scream of horror that cause all who hear it to shrivel inwardly.

✠ ✠ ✠

The second bandit's thoughts are little different from the first. But perhaps he has promised himself that what would be, would be, so he will not fight against the executioners—there is simply no use. He plans to be brave in his demeanor and take his impending torturous death "like a man." He has managed to borrow a little courage from his faint heart. In fact, he does quite well until that hellish moment his partner in crime loses his self-control and screams. It is that scream, like the howl of some poor animal caught in the hopeless jaws of a steel trap, that steals all his bravado. Instantly he feels himself go limp.

He studies the gallows on which his pitiful friend is hanging. Perspiration pops out in little drops of anguish all over his brow as he watches the soldiers make ready his own death. Some unseen wisp of frozen air seems to chill him, for he shudders convulsively. Then the soldiers come. He struggles violently. In one Herculean spasm of energy,

106

he seems almost certain to kick himself free, but soon he, too, is dying. He bites his lip to fight back a scream of terror, for there is a third man yet to die—Jesus of Nazareth.

But the third man to die is clearly no thief. It is as though he has for years studied the prospect of dying this horrible way and is completely and utterly resigned to it. He is not possessed by the panic and fear of the other two. The soldiers do not have to drag Jesus to his death. When the time comes, he walks resolutely to his cross and lies down on it.

Then, with a willingness that seems almost eager, he stretches out his left hand to the executioner. A black nail is placed at his wrist. The hammer man hesitates momentarily, and Jesus looks at him as if to say, "Suffer it to be so now, for so it must be to fulfill all righteousness!" And with that look of reassurance, the hammer falls on the spike with repeated blows until the hand is secured to the cross. Then this confident Nazarene stretches out his right hand and looks at the mallet man as if he is saying, "If a man shall spike thy left hand to the cross, offer to him the right hand also." Soon that hand, too, is fastened. The cross is wedged into the earth. . . .

Boldly silhouetted against the dawn that ugly April morning, the cross stood. People then asked what it meant. We are still asking what it means. The cross is both problematic and axiomatic for us. It is problematic because it defies human logic and reason. Its eternal intricacies escaped even the analysis of thinkers like Anselm and Aquinas. How can we with smaller minds ever apprehend its glory?

Axiomatically, the cross is central in Judeo-Christian history. All that precedes it is preparation. All that comes after it is consequence. It has become the theme of countless volumes, the subject of artistic masterpieces, the object of theological controversies. No one who believes in Christ and in his gospel can get along without the cross, for it is the strategic reason anyone believes in the first place. For here at the cross is where the founder of the Christian faith and any defender of that faith become introduced. Not only that, but every virtue of Christianity is present in the cross, and every sin is also there. In this strange mix, we confess that it was for us that his virtue must answer our sin.

If we would know love—real, selfless love—we must study the cross, this enigmatic tree of death. Sacrifice is there. So is forgiveness. Righteousness? Yes, it is there in abundance. Having studied the tree, perhaps we will gain an energized spirit of transformation.

We cannot say that the cross is an impersonal symbol, swept away by cascading decades of lawless, unorganized time. It is never this. It is for us! It is personal! Individual persons become involved with it. It is personal because it is the greatest need of persons who have never discovered it. It is personal because a person died there. It is personal because it can be owned by persons.

The cross confers on us the glorious attribute of belonging. It belonged to Jesus. It belonged to him long before the eighteenth year of Tiberius, the year in which he died. It was his long before the tree from which it was made was even a sapling. It belonged to him before the cosmos was framed. Long before God ever spangled the black canvas of night with a thousand glittering constellations, the cross belonged to Jesus.

And in the dim ages while God waited for our coming, the cross was already waiting, like a wooden savior to save us when the time came. Christ would meet us at the stake when we were in need of the serpent on the pole. When we were old enough to look, we could live. God, who sits above the ages and sees the past, present, and future at a single glance, had his saving grace stacked up in what he saw as the future storehouse of our need.

And, of course, Christ could not own the cross without owning the pain of rejection and disbelief. Can anyone really say whether rejection and loneliness are less painful than nails and ropes and thorns? The pain most severe to the Master may have been that anguish of human unbelief. These hurts are not assuaged with balms or diminished by narcotics. Out of the thousands who called him Lord, so few were at the cross. Except for one of his special Twelve, his mother, a judge named Nicodemus, and some gallant women from Galilee, there were no loyal faces in the mob. This rejection was so painful that he could but ask his Father, "Hast thou forsaken me [too]?"

The cross is his! He earned it by carrying it along the *Via Dolorosa!* It was literally the only thing the Lord had with him when he closed his eyes in death. It is uniquely his.

For none but Jesus of Nazareth has ever taught that one man might suffer—yes, even die—for all. The paradox of the cross belonged to Jesus; the cross is at once the greatest picture of love, yet the clearest portrait of hate. It is sublimely beautiful, yet stark, hideous, and ugly. It seems a waste of a good man, yet it is the salvation of bad men.

✝   ✝   ✝

It belonged to him to bequeath to us. What belonged to the Teacher was to belong to us. In fact, Jesus taught that unless we own the cross we cannot even be his disciples: "And anyone who does not carry his cross and follow me cannot be my disciple" (Luke 14:27 NIV). Cross-bearing is the imperative of our discipleship. It is easy to pick from a crowd those who are disciples, for they are the ones with the crosses on their shoulders.

A baptismal certificate tells you that you have been baptized. A form letter tells you that you are a church member. But only a cross borne on your back tells you that you are a disciple. If you have no cross, you are not a disciple.

✝   ✝   ✝

We have developed some strange concepts as to what cross-bearing really means. What did Jesus mean when he said that we should take up a cross? He was not referring to a dainty trinket dangling from a gold chain. Neither was he referring to a silver and ebony crucifix suspended at the end of a rosary. Nor did he mean a brazen cross carried in the processional of the Eucharist.

The cross is something vital we endure for the Lord of the kingdom. For Stephen, it was martyrdom. For Paul, it meant making his own defense before Nero. For Dietrich Bonhoeffer, it meant being hanged by the Nazis. For Jim Elliot, it was an inspired attempt to draw God's circle of love around savage tribesmen. For William Wallace, it was death in a communist prison cell.

It is wrong to refer to the trivial things of our lives as "our cross." That which one gives up for Lent is not a cross. A toothache is not a cross. The lack of some particular talent that would add energy or charm to one's personality is not a cross. Before we hastily designate anything as "our cross" and "our claim to discipleship," we must ask ourselves what a cross really is. We must look at *his* cross and then ask ourselves what we have offered him by way of sacrifice, humility, and obedience that measures up.

✠   ✠   ✠

We must ever free ourselves from that mistaken notion that crosses belong in the front of churches. Crosses belong on the back of Christians. Remember how happy Christian was in Bunyan's *The Pilgrim's Progress* when he finally came to the cross? He came to the cross and it felt wonderful! For the first time that he could remember, he could walk straight. The sins of a lifetime had bent him until life was burdensome. When he faced the cross of Christ, the burdens were lifted. He straightened up and walked away with a sprightly step. There was a new light and free energy about him. Christian's heavy load of guilt had all been taken away at the cross.

Soon he discovered, however, that God had only taken the sin from his back to replace it with a cross. The cross does not free us from sin so that we can live any way we wish and participate in any activity whatsoever. No, the cross removes the burdens of guilt that we carry so that we can be free to bear the cross itself.

✠ ✠ ✠

The kingdom of God has no citizens that are not cross-bearers. We must own the cross! How does the cross of Christ become ours? By realizing that we are involved with Jesus. We cannot share his triumph without sharing in his responsibility. We will never carry the cross unless somehow we become convinced that the cross on which Jesus died is the outcome of *our* sin. It is here that most would-be cross-bearers fail to make the grade. It seems such an illogical hurdle for the learner to leap. But Jesus was not killed just by some sinners who wore Roman armor or first-century Palestinian robes. The cross was not the finished product of sinners; it was the finished product of sin.

Jesus' untimely death was not just to deal with the sin of men who were his contemporaries. The crucifixion was God's dramatic answer to the sins of all humanity. The cross was raised in the sands of the first century, but its shadow falls the entire length of calendar time. The cross was lifted up to deal with the sins of Simon Peter, the sins of Augustine, the sins of Martin Luther, the sins of John Wesley, and our own sins. It is the answer to every century's cry for justification.

Yes, the cross belongs to us. It is the result of our sin. We cannot push the responsibility of the cross onto Pilate or Herod or Roman legionaries or Jewish priests. It is our deliverance, but also our crime! One Good Friday I wrote these lines:

"Not my sin, oh Lord," I cried,
  "that murdered God.
At Calvary the star of distant heaven
  bled—but not for my iniquity."

112

Christ said, "My son, the crime of time
   is your own felony.
For you the hate of planet earth
   fell heavy on me.

"It was because you needed life,
   My life was counted loss.
I was suspended from the tree
   and life dripped from my cross.

"And, although ebbing centuries
   have passed away since then,
you share this human homicide
   and need the world's Friend."

Have *you* taken up the cross? Perhaps, in the present starburst of technology and science, the cross seems antiquated. Perhaps you feel that the cross is a museum relic from man's superstitious past and should be laid aside in this bright new "post-Christian" era. Not possible! Our brave new world can never demonstrate its courage by laying aside the cross and continuing on without it.

✠ ✠ ✠

The cross is still relevant, even in an age when we hurl new stars into the night and program interplanetary travel. It is still the only hope of individuals, even in this noonday of human intellect and achievement. But it seems not to impress many in our age. It has many pretenders, but few defenders. This is no surprise to the disciples of Christ; for Jesus taught that the cross would be interesting to many, but vital to only a few. He predicted that many would be called, but few would be chosen (Matt. 22:14).

✠   ✠   ✠

Many have seen the cross, but few carry it. Some time ago, I went to see one of these "biblical" movies. Just before the intermission, the crucifixion was presented in breathtaking color and drama. The sounds of the hammer, ringing out upon the nails, echoed through the stereophonic speaker system of the theater; it was a frigid sort of clang that sent a shiver through the audience. Then the cross was lifted upright in the center of the wide screen. Behind the cross, the wide-angle camera swept the heavens.

Then the celluloid film projected a bright carbon incandescence, and the screen soon boiled with angry clouds made dark and heavy by rain. The soundtrack ricocheted the roll of ear-splitting thunder. After a raucous, sudden clap of thunder, the camera fell once more on the cross. Blood was beginning to run from the wound in one of Christ's hands. It ran red and vivid and bright on the dull, rough, brown wood and dripped over the crossbeam in a tiny rivulet. In the center of the cross, it was joined by another little stream, running from the wound in his other hand. That tiny ribbon of red continued on down the vertical wooden beam and began collecting in a depression at the foot of the cross.

Then the rain began to fall. The rain accumulated in that small basin and mingled with the red. Soon the pool filled to overflowing and began trickling down the mountainside. The small red rill combined with other torrents of rushing water. Finally it became a great crimson tide for this world's salvation—but, more than that, for *my* salvation.

It was magnificent. I was thunderstruck with the majesty yet the horror of Calvary. What a commanding portrayal of the pageant of redemption. Then, before I was ready to leave the scene, the film sequence stopped. The lights slowly illuminated the theater and filled it with a pale twilight.

✠ ✠ ✠

It took a moment or so for me to make the trip from Calvary back to the theater. But soon I found myself in the aisle, elbow to elbow with others in the audience, making my way to the lobby. I wondered if everyone had been as awestruck with the cross as I had been.

In the lobby, men laughed and chattered as though nothing had happened. Jewelry-bedecked women tossed their heads with lighthearted caprice. Children clamored for a drink at the water fountain. A noisy line formed at the concession booth. In the lounges, theater-goers used language that suggested the very antithesis of what they had just witnessed.

It was not that I had gone to that lobby expecting everyone to be collected into little prayer groups. Nor did I expect to find them singing "When I Survey the Wondrous Cross." Most people who see the cross are not impressed with it. They can see it and walk away and forget it. Yet, the Christian who sees the cross and esteems it is a person who understands his or her debt. He or she alone owns the cross.

✠ ✠ ✠

Ours is his sacrifice; his sacrifice is our debt. How far does this obligation of ours reach?

Paul seemed to believe that once we understand the price that Jesus paid to set us free, we truly are in debt. "Therefore, brothers, we have an obligation . . ." he said (Rom. 8:12 NIV), and the obligation stems from his gift of

115

salvation that was purchased at the cross. "I am obligated both to Greeks and non-Greeks, both to the wise and the foolish," said the apostle (Rom. 1:14 NIV). It is never enough to accept the finished work of Christ and spend the currency of his forgiveness totally on ourselves. The burden to share the cross and its message lay so hard upon Paul that he cried, "Woe be unto me if I preach not the gospel" (1 Cor. 9:16). Surely this wonderful salvation we own is not ours to hide and protect. It is given to us only to share until all the world we touch is as free as we are.

The obligation of the cross means that we whose sins demanded it now must admit that it is our forgiveness that also makes its demands. In keeping it for ourselves, we, the owners of the water of life, will see it stagnate and become unfit. Only as we pass on the water of life is it truly the water of life. It contains no life if we hoard it.

⚜ ⚜ ⚜

Arthur Blessitt has devoted his life to carrying the cross around the world. He has dragged it across the continents—from Africa to Asia, from Europe to North and South America. When I first learned of his devotion to the idea, I felt that he was a sensationalist, and that sooner or later his reputation would be rendered bogus. But, after seeing all his years of dedication to the project, I now believe that Arthur understands that he is obligated to portray this unforgettable image of discipleship.

Through the Sahara, across Arabia, through the jungles, and along the steppes. Through rain or sunshine and into the vast arenas where athletes compete, there is Arthur and his cross. His is a debt that owns him. His Christ cannot be shunted aside while Arthur merely lives as most of us do—going our separate ways, making a living, or (as in my case) writing books about our fever for the issue.

I only hope that the image of Arthur Blessitt's discipleship may settle into our consciousness until we freely admit that we are debtors. Once we totally acknowledge our debt, perhaps we will begin to repay it by the offering of ourselves. Then shall our lives sing with Sir John Bowring:

> In the cross of Christ I glory,
> Tow'ring o'er the wrecks of time,
> All the light of sacred story
> Gathers round its head sublime.[1]

*he hope which was
then entertained scarcely by
one thief on the cross is now
cherished by nations everywhere on earth, who are
marked with the sign of the
cross on which he died that
they may not die eternally.*

Augustine
The City of God

7

The Death of Death

Afraid of Neither Death nor Dying

*A*nd when Jesus had cried out again in a loud voice, he gave up his spirit. At that moment the curtain of the temple was torn in two from top to bottom. The earth shook and the rocks split. The tombs broke open and the bodies of many holy people who had died were raised to life. They came out of the tombs, and after Jesus' resurrection they went into the holy city and appeared to many people (Matt. 27:50–53 NIV).

"To die well is to die willingly," wrote Seneca. And so when I think of Christ at his execution, I must remember again that he said, "I lay down my life . . . and no man takes it from me" (John 10:17–18). Is it possible that he anticipated his own death? Was he not but thirty-three years old and in love with his Father's world? He was, and yet I believe that he did anticipate death.

It was the thought of dying that made the Master sweat great drops of blood in Gethsemane (Luke 22:44). There come those times that we would make a truce with dying. It often comes with torturous pain, and surely the cross was the prime example of what dying may require. Musetta Gilman understands that there are all kinds of crosses and that the dying is a killer of all humanity. She wrote on the death of her friend:

> I never thought that I
> Would make a truce with you,
> Oh, Death—
> Waxer of faces;
> Stealer of breath.
>
> But when I saw her bones
> Securely bound in linkless chain
> Victim of torture;
> Prisoner of pain;
> Her brilliant mind divorced
> From sight, from sound
> No longer free.
> Stalker at midnight,
> Keeper of key,
> You loosened her bond
> Restored dignity.[1]

Yet it is not with death that we would generally make the truce, but with dying. For most of us, I think, fear not the state of death; it is the final steps that lead into it that we most fear. Yet, how well Christ lives out the doctrine of Seneca—dying willingly and dying well.

Of what personal and individual significance is the crucifixion of a Nazarene rabbi? Where are we to probe for meaning to it all? Why does the untimely death of this young and gentle Jesus have more meaning than the death of other great men? Why should we regard him any more highly than Socrates, who obediently drank his hemlock? What has he done more praiseworthy than Joan of Arc, who humbly committed herself unto God from a flaming stake? Has his life been more fruitful, or his death more grieved, than India's courageous Gandhi?

Let us say simply that the cross stands for death. To be sure, it is a more dramatic kind of death than most people ever experience. Still, it is not the most horrible death ever endured. In fact, Jesus' crucifixion itself is not unique. One has only to observe the biographies of Antiochus the Seleucid or Nero the Emperor to see how very common crucifixions once were. Thousands of such executions came before the cross of Christ, and thousands came after it.

⊹ ⊹ ⊹

It even seems likely that Jesus was not the first person to die on the very cross that took his life. Crosses were gallows of execution and were probably used over and over again. Perhaps his very cross had been stained with the blood of a score of corpses before Jesus died there. Doubtless it was used for other executions after his own. It would have been as unthinkable to use a cross only once and throw it away, as it would have been for French "citizens" to use a guillotine only once and discard it, or for a state penitentiary to use an electrocution device for only one condemned prisoner.

121

Suffice it to say that Jesus' suffering was neither unique or inordinately longer than others'. Even the thieves who died beside him suffered longer than he did.

If all these things are true concerning the cross, why has the cross become the ensign and standard of Christianity? Remember, the cross stands for DEATH. It really represents two sorts of death: the death of a particular man named Jesus, who was called Christ, and the generic principle of "death" as it relates to all men. In short, his death and ours.

⊹   ⊹   ⊹

Death and dying have become a kind of preoccupation for the West. People who "have everything" think about death incessantly and try to analyze the concept. There was a day when we all spoke openly about death and guardedly of sex. Now we have somewhat reversed the tone and frequency of our conversations. Although death fills our cinemas and novels, we laugh a lot and fill our lives with incessant clowning and good times so that we can keep the wolves at bay.

But the cross has come to illustrate that death is not the error we had supposed. Jesus, dying in the most excruciating way, was not dead for long. In the chronicles of God, no death has ever lasted long. We fall asleep and awaken a world away. It is amazing just how often the New Testament speaks of death as sleep (Acts 7:60; 1 Cor. 11:30; 15:51; 1 Thess. 4:14). John Chrysostom in the fourth century said,

> What is death at most?
> It is a journey for a season:
> a sleep longer than usual.

122

If thou fearest death,
thou shouldst also fear sleep.[2]

Death is not only sleep; it is a sleep of transformation. Paul said, "We will not all sleep [or die], but we will all be changed" (1 Cor. 15:51 NIV). We all look forward to sleeping this wonderful sleep of transformation. Ben Franklin wrote this epitaph for his own gravestone:

> The body of
> Benjamin Franklin, Printer,
> Like the cover of an old book,
> Its contents torn out,
> And stript of its lettering and gilding,
> Lies here, food for worms;
> But the work shall not be lost,
> For it will, as he believ'd,
> Appear once more
> In a new and more elegant edition,
> Corrected and improved
> By the Author.[3]

✠ ✠ ✠

Jesus' own body was changed into a more transcendent body just by dying and receiving the resurrection nature. This is not to say he was changed into a perfect body, for he *was* perfect, but his body was changed in nature. He became the model of how death shall transform us as well: ". . . . For the trumpet will sound, the dead will be raised imperishable, and we will be changed. For the perishable must clothe itself with the imperishable, and the mortal with immortality" (1 Cor. 15:52–53 NIV). The cross is the lectern from which the world's great-

123

est teacher gave us lessons in how to take the final and most difficult step of our physical lives.

The cross is a more horrible kind of death to remember than if Jesus had simply died in bed from natural causes. We hail Golgotha as the terrible yet fascinating arena of our faith. It is more than interesting speculation that draws us, for here the vital areas of our faith become tied to the fury and the drama of his crucifixion. Some of the deepest lessons about death could be taught only by his dying. God could scarcely have made his teaching clear with anything less than Calvary.

God stood the cross up to remind us that death is the inevitable end of every physical life. The cross is singular evidence that even good men die. I once read about a good man who was told by his physician that he had an incurable malignancy and was going to die. He would not die at that moment, or perhaps even that month, but he would die. In his body he carried the sentence of death. The man was neither startled nor alarmed by the pronouncement. He knew that he could have said to the doctor who had issued the ultimatum, "You will die, too, Doc!" Or he might have said to the whole planet, "You, too, will die, world!" Death is the great inevitable statistic, cried George Bernard Shaw—one out of one must die.

✠ ✠ ✠

There is an ancient fable of Baghdad that tells of a merchant who sent his servant to the bazaar to purchase food. After only a few minutes, his servant came back and fell at his employer's feet. Blanched with fear, he begged, "A horse, a swift horse, please, master. Down at the market I bumped into a woman, and when she turned around and faced me I could see that woman was Death. She raised her arm to strike me, but I escaped her. Please, I must

124

have a horse—your fastest. I will escape Death by riding to Samarra."

The merchant loaned his slave his fastest horse and went back to the bazaar, where he, too, saw Death standing among the shambles. "Why did you terrorize my servant this morning?" the merchant asked Death.

"I didn't mean to terrorize your servant. Mine was only a reaction of surprise. I was astonished to see him here in Baghdad, for I have an appointment with him tonight in Samarra."[4]

✠ ✠ ✠

Death, indeed, is that land from which no traveler returns. We all must die. "It is appointed unto man once to die," says the Scriptures (Heb. 9:27). Nothing can prevent it!

The idea of ultimate and universal death is not just theological chitchat. C. G. Jung said it was our singular preoccupation after we reach the age of thirty-five. Biologists teach us that in all living organisms there exist two principles: anabolism, the building of protoplasm; and catabolism, the breakdown of protoplasm. When the former exceeds the latter, there is growth. When the two are held in balance, there is stabilization. But when catabolism begins to occur at a faster rate, there is gradual disintegration and death. In short, from the very moment of conception, our own death is inherently part of our passing physiology.

✠ ✠ ✠

Death is not a theological Frankenstein's monster created by power-mad theologians to scare unthinking individuals around to their viewpoint. Death is fact! It is a fact more unpleasant than life, but a fact that is just as certain as life and has a way of springing itself into all our unsuspecting moments. It becomes the grim reminder at every New Year's Eve party that we are not merely watching a clock, we are watching our passing.

Death is so unwelcome a terror that we have devised a whole new glossary of terms to avoid saying the word itself. If someone has died, we would rather phrase it "gone" or "passed away" or "departed" or "entered into peace" or "crossed over to the other side." Sudden death can have some violent synonyms, like "murder," "execution," and "homicide." But we prefer not to use those brutal synonyms more often than necessary. Death is never desirable; even the suicide does not choose it because it is filled with happy meaning, but because it seems less painful than living.

⌗   ⌗   ⌗

The purpose of this chapter is not to get people to adopt a futile "eat drink and be buried" concept of life and death. At the same time, however, it might well influence some to give up their unrealistic "I'll go on *ad infinitum*" philosophy of carefree existence. Death is an actuality. *Our* actuality! Infrequently it is anticipated willingly by those who have spent in anguish and pain the months and years preceding its arrival. But, for most of us, it is an unwelcome intruder, one that leaves Schubert's greatest symphony unfinished and renders Shakespeare's skull as meaningless as poor Yorick's.

⌗   ⌗   ⌗

And what has the cross to do with this inevitability? Has the cross abolished death? No, at least not biological death. Each time a heart ceases to beat and the pulse ceases its rhythmic swelling of wrist, the word *death* is spoken again. So the cross has not eliminated death, but it has redefined it.

Because of the cross, we are unafraid. For after Christ's cruel death he went to be with his Father. Indeed, he died saying to a thief, "Today, you will be with me in paradise" (Luke 23:43). It is the glorious triumph of his cross that announces that to be absent from the body is to be present with the Lord" (2 Cor. 5:8). Death is but the gateway to the automatic entrance into heaven. Now we know the truth of the matter. We but trade heartbeat for glory, and it will be most exciting. We shall go from the instant pain of our passing to the full presence of knowing the Lord face to face. "Hallelujah!" cries the spirit of that old Negro hymn:

> "Sit down, brother."
> "Can't sit down."
> "Sit down, brother."
> "Can't sit down."
> "Sit down, brother."
> "Can't sit down. I just got to Heaven
> And I can't sit down!"

✠   ✠   ✠

What is the definition of our life's end that issues from the cross? Our being and personality do not cease with our respiration and pulse. The cross says pointedly that true life has no end, and true death has never really known life. If we really have life, we can never know death—and if we ever experience death, we were always dead and never knew life.

127

To untangle this Gordian riddle, let us look at an example of death that confronted Jesus just weeks before his own death occurred. In the eleventh chapter of John's Gospel is the story of the man Lazarus who had died. Yet Jesus refused to refer to him as dead; instead he said he was asleep (John 11:11). Later, Jesus told Lazarus' sister Martha, "I am the resurrection and the life . . . whosoever liveth and believeth in me shall never die . . ." (vv. 25–26 KJV). According to what Jesus said here, there is a life to be lived that is free of death. It is the cross that has made such life possible.

✠ ✠ ✠

The Bible has always spoken of sin as the cause of death. In Ezekiel the Scriptures say, "The soul that sinneth, it shall die . . ." (Ezek. 18:20 KJV). The Bible indicates in the Book of Genesis that we were created to have eternal life, but we lost this life through disobedience. Therefore, from Adam to Jesus, sin continued to produce death, but the atonement of Jesus Christ was the answer to the human problem of hopelessness. Jesus' voluntary giving of himself was the death to end all death. Indeed, it was the death of death! Through God's great heart of love, Jesus showed us that his death was in some way representative. Jesus died for us! This knows no proof, but God meant for us to accept it and believe it as truth.

Since that windy April day on which Jesus died, no one has had to experience death; it is no longer mandatory. The death of Jesus Christ was the last death that ever had to occur. This is not theological double-talk. It is literally true. Death is a thing of the past for those wise enough to give themselves to Christ and lose themselves in the secure yet mysterious cross of life.

✠ ✠ ✠

Yes, the cross has redefined death. No longer is death to be feared. In Jesus Christ we can understand that death is the end of nothing except physiological processes. Paul of Tarsus reminded us that death has had all of its sting removed. The great apostle phrased it this way: "Death is swallowed up in victory. O death, where is thy sting? O grave, where is thy victory?" (1 Cor. 15:54b–55).

This beautiful metaphor of death's inability to sting us can be drawn from the parallel idea that once an insect stings, it leaves in the flesh of its victim its envenomed weapon. Now it may fly on and carry along its ugly grudge to hurt and destroy, but its power is gone. Thus did death, the ancient destroyer, meet Jesus at the cross and sink into God's Son the last of its venom. Now death's reign of terror is over. Like an impoverished insect, it may buzz about us as if to instill the poison it has abandoned, but we know the truth. Death left its venom at the cross. The sting is gone.

✠ ✠ ✠

Paul could hardly be classed as a morbid person, and yet it is certainly true that he looked forward to death. This ecstasy with which he anticipated death may seem to some to be a false enthusiasm, but it was not. Paul gives his real feelings concerning life and death in Philippians:

> For, as I passionately hope, I shall have no cause to be ashamed, but shall speak so boldly that now as always the greatness of Christ will shine out clearly in my person, whether through my life or through my death. For to me life is Christ, and death gain; but what if my living on in the body may serve some good purpose? Which then

am I to choose? I cannot tell. I am torn two ways: what I should like is to depart and be with Christ; that is better by far; but for your sake there is greater need for me to stay on in the body (Phil. 1:20–24 NEB).

What the apostle says is that living in Christ is wonderful, but dying in Christ is magnificent. "To die is gain" (v. 21 NIV) is a glorious truth. One of Christianity's greatest truths is that all of us who believe are better off dead!

Paul had come to know this deathless living in Jesus Christ. He had discovered it to be the outcome of the cross. Although I will discuss self-sacrifice in the next chapter, I will introduce the idea in this important context. Paul had been to the cross; there he had come to know his Savior and had given himself in such a depth of surrender that he claimed: "I am crucified with Christ: nevertheless I live . . ." (Gal. 2:20 KJV).

In effect, Paul was saying that he only began to live when he had crucified himself. He said that life in its abundance and eternal power had come to him only when he had put to death his own ego, ambition, and will.

It is impossible to kill what is already dead. That is why Paul counsels us to reckon ourselves "dead to sin but alive in Christ" (Rom. 6:11). The key to not fearing death is to die ahead of time! Most people come up to the black horizon that marks the boundary of physical life and there they plant their heels in the sand and fiercely struggle against going on over. But here and there are those who "reckon themselves dead"—their worldly desires are gone. Their treasure is not in earthly banks, but is already stored in heaven (Matt. 6:20). What they own here has been given away. Their rich inheritance has gone on ahead of them and beckons powerfully. Because they have already died, they are unafraid.

✠   ✠   ✠

God had helped Paul to pull from his own selfish existence those parts of his life that were all for himself. This amounted to a day-by-day splitting off from Paul's life the old secular and earthbound personality that was filled with delusions of grandeur and always clamoring for self-recognition. There was an imaginary but substantial cross on which the new Paul was nailing the old one.

The old Paul was on the cross, but the new Paul felt this was good enough for him. The old Paul had too long been the only Paul. The new Paul considered trivial the desires for petty human recognition, the constant haggling for the chief seats in the halls of men, and all the other things that once seemed so primary and basic. Out of this struggle between the Pauls came both a crucifixion and a life that would never know death. A life that was, in fact, immune from death.

✠   ✠   ✠

The doctrine of the cross is not that we will live after we die, but that we will never have to die. The cross of Christ proclaimed the profound and precious paradox that death was dead. All of the New Testament that comes after the cross uses Jesus' term of "sleep" for those who reach the end of life. Death is an impossible threat for anyone who discovers the life that emanates from the cross.

The life-and-death message of the cross is such an intricate paradox that it defies human analysis. The claims of the atonement have been probed by the logic of many great minds, but it is still a mystery. The cross speaks in

131

mysterious syllables to let us know that Christ could not have given us life without giving up his own.

Jesus indicated that unless a grain of wheat falls to the ground and ceases to live, it can never reproduce itself. The life of the new plant can only grow out of the death of the seed. Life always grows out of death. As Peter Marshall wrote:

> The acorn cannot save itself,
>   if it is to bud a tree.
> The soldier cannot save himself,
>   if he is to save his country.
> Nor can the Shepherd save himself,
>   if he would save his sheep.[5]

⌗   ⌗   ⌗

Listen to the words that blazed with mockery from one of those little souls who stood before the cross: "He saved others; himself he cannot save" (Matt. 27:42a). But are not those words true? If death was to die and life was to really live, Jesus *had* to die.

God could not save his Son if he was to save us. The question of death as it pertained to Jesus and us was not a "both" issue. God could not save both his Son and us. It was an "either-or" matter. God could save *either* his beloved Son *or* his other beloved children.

⌗   ⌗   ⌗

The cross is a crisis of love. In his book *The Fall*, Albert Camus tells of such a terrible quandary. Camus has his hero, Jean-Baptiste Clamence, say: "Do you know that in my little village, during a punitive operation, a German officer courteously asked an old woman to please choose which of her two sons would be shot as a hostage? Choose!—can you imagine that? That one? No, this one!"[6] The picture this suggests is that of a mother trapped between her love for her two sons. She runs between them, embracing them, trying to make a hellish choice, for she has been told that she can save one of them, but not both. Here is a soul-rending crisis of love. Such a crisis ripped into the heart of divine love at the cross. Either we or Christ must die. For all his love, God cannot save both.

✠   ✠   ✠

This whole shattering dilemma is reminiscent of an illustration I once heard. I suspect this story is only fiction, but its dramatic phraseology speaks of a conflict between duty and love. According to the fable, a certain engineer regulated a revolving span across a mighty river. The bridge span was so constructed that it swung on an immense steel pin to allow for the passage of tugs and barges and other river traffic. When the span was closed, it was part of the roadbed of an important and busy railway. During all his years of employment, the engineer was responsible for opening the span for river traffic and closing it for lumbering freight trains and sleek silver streamliners with their cargoes of passengers. The daily life of the bridge engineer focused on the little control house filled with switches and levers that he knew and understood. Outside the house was a huge machine geared with immense cams and cogs whose monstrous steel teeth provided the power that swung the span back and forth over the river.

There came a day, so the parable continues, that the engineer took his young son to work with him. It was an exciting day in the boy's life. With fascination he hurled question after question at his dad. He had to know about the lights and the fuse panels and the levers and the machinery all at once. But it was not until the span had swung open to allow the passage of a stream of barges that it suddenly occurred to the engineer that his son was no longer in the control house.

The father's pulse quickened as he looked down. There was nothing below except the cold, gray, concrete pier, disappearing into a river churned white by the passing traffic. Then he looked out and spied his son playing in the machinery; he was inspecting it like a government official and passing his chubby little grease-smudged hands over the armatures and shafts. The engineer was about to go out and get the boy so he could swing the span shut, when a flashing light brought to his attention the approach of a passenger train.

There was no time to retrieve his son. The span must be closed. The father's heart leaped when he realized that his son would be crushed in the gears of that Herculean machinery. The ugly crisis demanded an ugly decision. Either his son would die, or a streamliner filled with hundreds of people would be doomed. With firm purpose the engineer reached for the closing lever.

As the streamliner flashed past the control house on the bridge, the engineer noticed the laughing and happy faces of the passengers through his anguished tears. In the club car they drank and ate and played cards. Elsewhere they read and relaxed and talked. Their blind detachment seared the heart of the father, who must henceforth live with the awareness that his son had died, and there was no one to notice or care.

Humanity's greatest sin lies in its indifference to the high cost that God paid to abolish death. Only the death of his Son was currency enough to pay the price. At Calvary, God realized he could not save both us and his Son. With a firm purpose he reached for the switch that operated the machinery of crucifixion.

God's Son was crushed in the gears of human violence and hatred. But from his cross issued our own life, free forever of the necessity of dying. This wonderful, fantastic, deathless living can be ours. Thanks to the cross, death has died.

*To have faith
is not part
of human nature,
but it is part
of human nature
that man's mind should go
against his inner instinct.*

Thomas Aquinas
Summa Theologica

8

The Dying Life

The Art of Sacrificing Ourselves

ater, knowing that all was now completed, and so that the Scripture would be fulfilled, Jesus said, "I am thirsty." A jar of wine vinegar was there, so they soaked a sponge in it, put the sponge on a stalk of the hyssop plant, and lifted it to Jesus' lips. When he had received the drink, Jesus said, "It is finished." With that, he bowed his head and gave up his spirit (John 19:28–30 NIV).

I have been crucified with Christ and I no longer live, but Christ lives in me. The life I live in the body, I live by faith in the Son of God, who loved me and gave himself for me (Gal. 2:20 NIV).

When every second counted, the Master's time was running out. In a little while the setting sun would look down and pronounce him dead. He had lived all of his life for this Friday. Now it was here. The ropes were cutting with purple savagery into his flesh. His wounded hands were numb. His head slumped forward on his chest, and sweat, mingled with blood, ran into the corners of his eyes, stinging them with temporary spasms of blindness. This was the end of Jesus' life!

Joseph Wittig once said, "A man's biography ought really to begin not with his birth but with his death; it can be written only from the point of view of its end, because only from there can the whole of his life in its fulfillment be seen."[1] So it is that when we tell anyone of Jesus we must begin with his death. One cannot even begin to understand the life of Christ without understanding his death. It is here at the cross that his biography begins.

Self-sacrifice is the fearsome way to say "self-denial." But neither word should be seen as making us grander than we really are. Both words really refer to the way we use our days, how we spend the small coins with which we buy the years of our lives. Anticipating our dying times keeps us remembering that life is inherently serious. Since, as the wag reminds us, "We cannot get out of life alive," we must let our impending death teach us how to spend the currency of our days.

And how are we to do it? Well, the apostle Paul said that he was "being poured out as a drink offering" (Phil. 2:17a). Indeed, *all* human life is being poured out, either in self-concern or in service. But it is the judgment of the cross that we should give our lives as a sacrifice to our Lord, who gave his life as a sacrifice for us.

We seldom react appropriately when we see a cross. We fail to make the correct response to this symbol of

Jesus' death, primarily because it seems to us an over-wrought, though underlived, representation of Christianity. Most people, on seeing a cross, immediately associate it with the triviality of church membership or pious rhetoric. Very infrequently does the mere sight of a cross stir a human heart with thoughts of the saving death of Jesus Christ. Even less frequently does it challenge even Christians to the giving of their lives.

The cross, alas, has degenerated into a near-vacuous symbol of a religious fraternity. Just as the compass and square stand for Freemasonry or the three links of chain stand for the Independent Order of Odd Fellows, so the cross stands for Christianity. For most people, it is a means of identification with a cause, but that's all!

It is a human fault that we have no in-depth reaction to the sight of the cross, though our world has literally gone "cross crazy." Celluloid crosses are manufactured for bookmarks. They are painted on automobile bumpers and displayed in plastic on dashboards. Luminous crosses are suspended on light pulls. They are worn on neck chains, embroidered on pulpit garments, welded to steeples, and built of polished wood for church altars. There are even factories that manufacture crosses on a production-line basis. We have "crucified" the cross with overexposure!

✠ ✠ ✠

We must see the cross anew as a rough piece of wood that spelled torture for Jesus Christ. This Jesus was not a figure of silver hung on polished ebony. He was a man condemned to a slow death. He was not created to be a crucifix of cold, unfeeling metal, but a human being whose blood oozed out into the chilling winds of an April morning in the third decade of the first century. It is not what the cross *was* to Jesus, but what it *is* to us that is so crucial (even this word *crucial* derives from the cross). Any man who cannot see the cross in this light is likely outside redemption's grasp.

We should direct our attention to the real issue of self-surrender. We should not "give ourselves" as an act of heroism during which we are all too conscious of our "sacrifice." Rather than phrasing our surrender as a negative, we must make it altogether in the positive mode. It is not that we herald our "giving up," but that we are absorbed in a positive passion of living for Christ. Consider the counsel of Psalm 27:4 (NIV):

> One thing I ask of the LORD,
>   this is what I seek:
> that I may dwell in the house of the LORD
>   all the days of my life,
> to gaze upon the beauty of the LORD,
>   and to seek him in his temple.

John White counsels us: "It is time we threw spiritual pragmatism out of the window. . . . It is time we forgot about our spiritual performance and our spiritual needs and gave ourselves up to passion."[2]

✠ ✠ ✠

We often make spiritual submission and self-crucifixion seem a negative and frightening affair. We call out to the needy, "Come to Jesus, dear sister or brother, and you will have a fine time being scorned, spurned, rejected, and living a miserable life. It will be just wonderful being despised, you'll see!" We ought not be as shocked as we are that "dungeon, fire and sword" are not exciting calls to our contemporaries.

Rather, the glory of effective self-crucifixion is not found in an act we have chosen so as to demonstrate how self-less we are. It is in reality a state we arrive at as the result of our passion for Christ. We are so in love with him that the ardor drives us with enough vitality that we become lost in his service. It is only when we stop to look back over our shoulders that we see a rut plowed in the sand by the cross we were bearing; for the joy of it, we had not noticed its weight. *Truly his burden is light and his yoke is easy* (Matt. 11:30).

Those who remain too conscious of their submission have experienced it in only surface ways. I once commented in *If This Be Love* that my mother raised us to own such a passion for life that we were suddenly surprised in mid-adolescence to realize we were poor. It was not a deception she intended to foster on us. It was just that her basic definition of life was "wealth." But the key thing I learned in mid-adolescence was not that we had been poor all our lives, but rather that those who considered themselves wealthy did so on the basis of such little things as bank accounts and certificates of deposit.

⁑   ⁑   ⁑

It is the positive passions that are the only worthy passions. It was years before I learned that a certain woman in our church had given her son one of her kidneys so that he could live. When I saw his scarred abdomen as we dressed after a racquetball game, I could only gasp, "What happened to you?" He smiled and told me that his mother bore his very set of scars; and without her scars, he could not live. I suddenly was dumbfounded, not so much by his scars or even his words, but by his smile. I noticed that she smiled a lot, too. And, of course, her passion would admit to no sacrifice. Joy is greater than pain. What is given up is no sacrifice between lovers. So should we feel about Jesus.

Our cross, his cross: these are the symbols of lovers, that's all. Yet to look on the cross reminds us that cheap grace is out of the question. He gave, we gave; and we have received as he received. He died and gloried in the dying that he might present us to his Father (John 17:24). We die and glory in the dying that our love might consume us with the only meaning possible in an unfeeling universe. God, sear our eyes and prevent us from weeping at the little we have given. The vast treasure of the cross overwhelms our petty charity.

It is for this important reason that George MacLeod has written:

> I argue that the cross be raised again at the center of the marketplace as well as on the steeple of the church. I am recovering the claim that Jesus was not crucified in a cathedral between two candles, but on a cross between two thieves; on the town garbage heap; at a crossroads so cosmopolitan that they had to write his title in Hebrew and Latin and in Greek; at the kind of place where cynics talked smut and thieves cursed, and the soldiers gambled. Because that is where he died, and that is what he died about, and that is where churchmen should be and what churchmanship should be about.[3]

The cross that ended Jesus' life is important; a cross that stands for anything else is trivial.

Ernest Hemingway wrote a book of short stories called *Men Without Women*. One of the stories included in that book is called "Today Is Friday." It is written in the form of a trilogy and deals with three Roman soldiers who have just crucified a Nazarene carpenter. After they have crucified this carpenter, who had claimed to be the Son of God, they stop by a tavern in ancient Jerusalem on the way back to the barracks.

One of the soldiers has been unaffected by the whole incident and drinks his ale as lustily as ever. Another of the soldiers just cannot forget this carpenter—he seemed like such a good fellow—but he orders himself a cup of ale and begins to drink it anyway. The third soldier is slapped on the back and told to order his ale and drink it. But he cannot. His heart and mind are still back there at the scene of the cross and on the man who was dying there.

While his raucous buddies chug-a-lug their ale, the third soldier keeps staring with a faraway look in his eyes and finally says, "He sure looked good in there today." Then there is more laughter and more table talk in the tavern. But ever and anon in the midst of ale and gaiety, the thunderstruck soldier says again, "He sure looked good in there today!"

Hemingway's story is not historical, but the reactions of these soldiers parallel some of the typical reactions of those who study the cross. The great mass of people go through life untouched by its importance. Not many have the sense and sobriety of that serious soldier who said, "He sure looked good in there today." Hemingway correctly pictures variant opinion and reaction to the cross. At the crucifixion there were mainly either those who reacted negatively to the cross itself, those who ignored what was happening, or those who merely watched in idle curiosity.

143

Few had a truly positive response to the cross and what it meant. Let us consider the three most common reactions to the cross of Jesus . . .

╬ ╬ ╬

There have always been, first of all, what we might call "the enemies of the cross." These were the people who actually despised the cross and its message and looked on both with scorn. It seems unthinkable that the cross, the epitome of love and sacrifice, could have enemies, but such was the case and still is. Paul realized that many hated the cross, and it was with a broken heart that he had to write to the church at Philippi and say, "For many walk, of whom I have told you often, and now tell you even weeping, that they are the enemies of the cross of Christ" (Phil. 3:18 KJV).

Many have despised the cross. There are always those in every age who will throw rocks at lions as long as they are in cages. These people were at the cross also. They had captured for themselves a heretic, and they were making the most of it. They circled the cross in scorn. Their mocking, hollow words will be an indictment against them on Judgment Day.

These enemies never sought to see any purpose in the cross; they were too busy hurling hate and slander at Jesus (Matt. 27:39–43). One can imagine the hollow ring of their sarcasm: "Jesus, we have every confidence that you are what you say you are—the Son of God! Why don't you come down from the cross and silence our insults?" Listen to the slurs that were likely directed at his teaching: "You claimed that you created the world. It seems like someone whose hands had created the world could pull three nails and come down. Or are you so comfortable you prefer to stay?" Then someone might have hurled an insult at his kingship: "Your Majesty, King of kings! Is God your father, as you have said? Your father seems awfully unconcerned about his naked, bleeding son!"

╬ ╬ ╬

There are still many today who would sneer at the defenders of the cross. They would say that we are wasting our devotion when we give it to a man crucified between two desperados. To many of the enemies of the cross, Jesus was little more than a quack faith-healer, an imposter. Communists, who once controlled almost half of this world's people, have traditionally been enemies of the cross. In our day, atheistic and agnostic philosophers are its enemies, too.

Yet the people in our time who are critical of the cross, and thus scornful of the atonement of Jesus Christ, are not a new race. It was their ancestors who looked with contempt on the cross so long ago. These enemies of the cross said they nailed Jesus there for his blasphemous teachings. Then, when his execution was under way, they committed the same kind of sacrilege of which they had falsely accused him. All enemies of the cross are always in the business of blasphemy. They forever downgrade his sacrifice, love, and divinity.

In considering the reactions to the cross, I am always reminded of the two classes of atheists. Some atheists say there is no God; others may declare there is, yet they allow him to make no functional difference in their lives. In a similar way, there are really two kinds of enemies of the cross: those who mock the suffering Christ, and those who bless his sacrificial dying but never take up a cross of their own in self-surrender. The cross is insulted less by its declared enemies than by its pretended friends. As far as I know there is only one meaningful way to sing "The Old

Rugged Cross": I must bear my own cross if I would be convincing to others.

Self-sacrifice is the chief issue of discipleship. Most of us Christians lay our "all on the altar" for Christ, only to find that in moments of stress our reluctant egos have crawled off the altar. And while we are so deviously committed, should we call ourselves friends or enemies?

✠ ✠ ✠

The *declared* enemies of the cross (in our land, at least) are not so common as those who somehow realize the cross is important but, because of its demands, merely sum up its attributes and ignore it, as perhaps even that second soldier did. These are "the undeclared," like the dicers at the crucifixion who, in the moment of that great drama, were casting lots for Christ's clothing. The dicers at Calvary had a good game going, a chance to win. And winning, to the dicers, is all, so they must not be interrupted for decision making.

If it were possible to return, by way of H. G. Wells' fabled time machine, to history's greatest moment, I would like to go back to Golgotha just long enough to interrupt those who gambled at the foot of the cross and ignored the gift of grace being offered them. Oh, for the opportunity to grasp those who played with dice and say to them, "Stop this game, you fools. Don't you realize that the issue of your own souls is being determined just a few feet above your heads? The Christ of Life is dying while you play!" In that majestic moment of redemption, the gamblers whiled away their opportunities. The dicers at Calvary were narcissists who had grown so callous in their own pursuits that they could neither see nor understand the whole issue of self-sacrifice being enacted in their midst.

✠ ✠ ✠

Are we really any wiser? Do we not still ignore the cross and focus all our attention on petty things? We have ears, yet are deaf to the utterances of the Christ impaled on our behalf. We have eyes, yet never look up to see the face of our Redeemer. Spiritually we are playing dice at the foot of the cross. We have our bingo societies and bowling leagues. We have bridge clubs and golf classes. We have our nightclubs, sports cars, and cocktail parties. Life for us is one grand whirl of confetti and ticker tape.

If we ever do try to arrest human attention long enough to tell others of the cross, they brush us aside. Frankly, most in our generation prefer to ignore it because of what it requires as a response. When we will not offer ourselves on the altar, we find that the secular Everest, which we thought we could conquer, has defeated us instead. Then, we find, we are not managing life. Life is managing us. We are completely manipulated by the roster of trivial activities we have charted for ourselves. We are tied down with a thousand lilliputian threads and become the victims of our own schedules.

✠ ✠ ✠

As we lay self-surrender aside, we become dicers, too absorbed in the game of life to stop and ponder the issues of repentance and faith. Occasionally we seem to sense that all our worldly importance and busyness is adding up to zero, but we will not stop to discover the gift of life. We are gambling at the foot of the cross. Few of us react negatively to the cross, as did its long-ago blasphemous enemies. In fact, we do not react to it at all! If the cross is a take it or leave it situation, we prefer simply to leave it.

I have elsewhere written that the most potent threat to Christianity never comes from those who blatantly attack its truths. The greatest danger always comes from those who become ensnared in the creeping tentacles of secularity and drawn into the jaws of the beast. We never march purposefully into hell; we fall asleep and slide in and raise ourselves from the stupor only when we pass the maw, noticing at last that we are lost irretrievably. The secular thrall is the final snare of the dicers, the undeclared players who gamble with their lives but never sacrifice them to any meaningful end.

✠   ✠   ✠

Calvary reveals a third reaction to the crucifixion. The Scriptures mention a group of people who quietly observed what was happening: "And sitting down, they watched him there" (Matt. 27:36). These "watchers of the cross" did not seem violently opposed to Jesus as were his enemies. Neither were they ignoring him like the gamblers, for they were watching. Some might even have been favorably impressed with the man on the cross, as was Hemingway's third soldier.

The crucifixion happened on a busy market day when many people were doubtless coming into the city to do their last-minute shopping for the Passover holidays. This was such an important Jewish holiday that the city was thronged with pilgrims returning to the Holy Land from every province of the Roman Empire. The cross had likely drawn an international crowd of onlookers. They were not completely disinterested, for they had stopped to watch. Yet they were not interested in becoming any more involved than this, either.

These watchers saw it all. They watched the condemned man being spiked. They saw the cross as it was jolted upright in its socket. They heard the dull thud it made when it fell into its hole. They saw Jesus try in vain to find a way to make his head comfortable against the rugged timber of the cross.

The last ravages of human existence involve trying to be comfortable while we die. Even those who crucify themselves in self-surrender struggle to find some way to hang conveniently while the unyielding wood makes no place for them to cradle their heads.

Submission is always uncomfortable work, but it is the grand virtue. St. Theresa wrote long ago: "They deceive themselves who imagine union with God consists in ecstasies, visions, the joys of sensible devotions."[4] Submission is grand identity with Christ, who confessed that he had nowhere to lay his head (Matt. 8:20). Nowhere is the loneliness, the homelessness, the restlessness of our self-crucifixion more obvious than at the dying place.

Why is it that those who often start out as pastors or television evangelists often find their self-sacrifice gradually being replaced by the good life? "All to Jesus, I Surrender," is a hymn so easily replaced by, "Lord, Please Buy Me a Mercedes-Benz." Because the two songs are in the same musical key, it's sometimes hard to tell when we've changed either the melody or our commitment. I believe that most of the three-private-jets preachers never intended to luxuriate in the donations, but the cross gradually grew so uncomfortable that they abandoned it along the way.

Rabbi Kushner commented that we can only become useful to society when we become like hunting dogs who learn to bring back the game birds in their mouths without taking a bite of them.[5] How true this is for all of us who want to live the crucified life. When God dumps his blessings upon us, it is an easy stretch to start living for the blessings rather than for God. When we finally return the prize to the Master, the prize we should have delivered whole has been half-eaten. And we say at such moments, "The laborer is worthy of his hire." Or, as Father Divine used to say, "Seek ye first the kingdom of God and all these [material] things will be added unto you" (see Matt. 6:33).

Herein lies the greatest snare of the crucified life. People who honor God will often be admired for "clothing themselves in Christ" (Gal. 3:27). The trick is to live in the midst of admiration and not stop overlong before our dressing mirrors. To turn the light on Christ is to notice that a bit of it spills over on ourselves. But soon it is not focused mainly on Christ, but on us *and* Christ. Later it falls only on us, while Christ waits in the wings. Crucifying ourselves is therefore daily. If we forget on Tuesday, on Wednesday we might not think of it again.

✝ ✝ ✝

Chesterton wrote of the man we now call St. Francis of Assisi. On returning from the crusades that should have but did not make him shrink in fear, he was stopped, chilled at the heart, by a leper in the road:

Francis Bernardone saw his fear coming up the road towards him; the fear that comes from within and not without; though it stood white and horrible in the sunlight. For once in the long rush of his life his soul must

150

have stood still. Then he sprang from his horse, knowing nothing between stillness and swiftness, and rushed on the leper and threw his arms around him. It was the beginning of a long vocation of ministry among many lepers, for whom he did many services; to this man he gave what money he could and mounted and rode on. We do not know how far he rode, or with what sense of the things around him; but it is said that when he looked back, he could see no figure on the road.[6]

Kissing lepers is, of course, acceptable only to those who have already died to Christ. When we find any contagion repugnant or beneath the dignity of what Christ asks us to do, we are still too much alive to our own self-interests.

I have never loved the scriptural Jesus more than when he faces the man who was possessed by a "legion of demons" (Mark 5:1–20). The fearsome monster, who had maimed and injured others, is restored to wholeness by the Christ whose life was not his own. I see the Master embracing this poor man, for Jesus lived totally for the Father, and hugging madmen, like kissing lepers, was a threat of no consequence.

Our witnessing is gloriously freed by our surrender. Chesterton also sees that in the wonderful moment of Francis's conversion. The man of Assisi stood to say, "Up to this time I have called Pietro Bernardone father, but now I am the servant of God." He then piled his garments in a heap on the floor, except for his hair shirt, and walked out into the snow. Penniless and parentless, without any support or family ties, and bathed only in the mercy of his own submission, he walked off in renunciation of his once lavish life. But as he passed under the frosted trees, "he burst suddenly into song."[7]

In Zeffirelli's wonderful movie, as Francis walks away from the wealthy watchers of Assisi, he declares simply, "I am born again." The crowd pities him, but Francis is jubilant. The cross had given him a reason to live, and the disdain that marked the faces of the onlookers was refuted by the song of freedom that set him singing in the snow.

✠   ✠   ✠

When it comes to crosses, some watch and some die to self. Those who merely watch are buried in unmarked graves; those who die change the world and—though it is never their ambition—they are celebrated for the cross they carried in their hearts.

So it was, of course, at Calvary. In watching Jesus die, a smug, self-satisfied feeling came over the crowd. They felt good about themselves, for they were not the ones who were driving the nails that day. They would not have flogged Jesus or ringed his brow with thorns. Such inhumane things belonged to the cruel men who had charge of the crucifixion. They only watched.

And they felt innocent! Were they? A similar situation, which is wholly imaginary but possible, is that of a young boy playing in the road, with an automobile bearing down on him. You know it will soon take his life, but he is not *your* child, and it is not *your* fault that he is playing in the highway. So you merely watch, and soon the child is bleeding and dead. Although no court in the country could possibly hold you responsible, you cannot help blaming yourself. You should have given a cry of alarm. Or you might have rushed out into the highway and made an attempt at rescue. You should have done something more than merely looking on. Are you not guilty?

✠ ✠ ✠

The entire idea of being crucified with Christ mandates that true Christianity can afford no mere onlookers. Those who take up their cross have said, "The tomb I choose, wherein I reckon myself dead to sin, symbolizes my commitment. Now I am alive in Christ" (see Rom. 6:11). In the Iran/Iraq war, on the Thursday before the battle began, the Iraqi soldiers dug 40,000 graves in the lonely desert sands. They did not dig these graves for the enemies they hoped to slaughter, but for themselves. These holes signified their commitment to die for the cause. That they never used them is glorious, but I think not so glorious as the fact that in their minds they were committed to the death. Bonhoeffer was right. Jesus' call to "take up the cross" (Luke 9:23) was really his way of saying, "Come with me and die." Commitment to the way of the cross is not just the pledge of martyrs, it is the password to heaven. Only a dying life is a Christian life.

This same yardstick must be applied to watchers of the cross. When the Son of God died, none of them could be classified as innocent. There were enough onlookers, in all likelihood, to have prevented the cross by brute strength. Any who stand by and do nothing to prevent injustice become guilty of the injustice themselves. Yet there is always this purely human attempt to shift the blame to someone else. So the watchers at Calvary felt a great deal better by telling themselves that the guilt for the crime belonged to the execution squad.

A parallel might be drawn in our own society. A condemned man sits in an electric chair, although there is much reason to doubt he is guilty of any crime. At five minutes till midnight the electrocutioner, hooded in black,

153

enters the room. At midnight he walks to the circuit breaker and closes the switch. There is the sizzling of electrodes. There is the crackling sound of high voltage and heavy current. A man is dead—and perhaps he was innocent!

The man under the black hood must rationalize his actions if he is to maintain any mental stability. So he reasons that *he* has not really taken a life; the electricians who spliced those intricate circuits were to blame. Those who wired the apparatus maintain it was the judge who was responsible, for he or she handed down the sentence. The judge insists that blame rests with the jury who handed down the verdict. The jury excuses itself and points to the laws of the state, which (at least in theory) represent the will of the people. Who is responsible for the execution? Well, just about everybody, it seems.

So it was, too, at Christ's execution site. The watchers of the cross were as guilty of his death as the hammer man. Their own failure to act in a positive way has condemned them. They also have descendants, however. There are many in our day who insist that Calvary happened so long ago that they cannot possibly be implicated in the awful crime committed there. When we allow this claim to stand, we fail to understand that the cross has *no* innocent bystanders. If we merely *watch* the cross, our eyes may see, but our hearts are blind.

We are all guilty, if only because of our insensitivity. God lost all that he held dear on that cross. But we twentieth-century cross-watchers are often so self-absorbed that we never feel any pity about this, much less shame. When we will not weep over the heartbreak that God experienced in the first century, we are guilty of the cross through our ugly, leaden unconcern. We must give up our stance of innocence and accept full responsibility for the cross. We must apologize for our sins or we will forever forfeit eternity with Christ.

"God so loved the world that he gave his only Son." The cost of the project was so immense, that there can be none who claim the cross without owning its demands. It is impossible to honor the Lord's surrender to his cross without surrendering to our own.

Let us claim for our champion that nameless centurion who was gripped by the commanding majesty of Jesus Christ and confessed in choked emotion, "Surely he was the Son of God!" (Matt. 27:54 NIV). Truly, he *was* the Son of God! Total commitment bled into the fibers of the cross. It is his dying! It is ours! May his precious blood color our dull lives with a willingness to sacrifice our all.

*That glorious form,
that Light insufferable,*

*That far beaming blaze
of majesty, . . .*

*He laid aside,
and here with us to be,*

*Forsook the courts
of everlasting day,*

*And chose with us
a darksome house of clay.*

John Milton
Paradise Regained

9

The Piercing of Pain

The Triumph of the Cross in Our Suffering

rom the sixth hour until the ninth hour darkness came over all the land. About the ninth hour Jesus cried out in a loud voice, "Eloi, Eloi, lama sabachthani?"—which means, "My God, my God, why have you forsaken me?"

When some of those standing there heard this, they said, "He's calling Elijah."

Immediately one of them ran and got a sponge. He filled it with wine vinegar, put it on a stick, and offered it to Jesus to drink. But the rest said, "Leave him alone. Let's see if Elijah comes to save him" (Matt. 27:45–49 NIV).

There is a demon that stalks us or holds us at bay and terrorizes us. Pain is its name. With our entire nervous system at pain's caprice, we live in dread of the day that it will have its way with us. Years ago the popular entertainer Arthur Godfrey commented on his bout with cancer by saying, "One day I never felt better in my life and then, Boom! This horrible, skulking thing visible only as a ghostly shadow on an x-ray negative—this 'thing' that no longer gives me pain, probably because I cannot feel it through the cold, clutching fear that is gnawing at my vitals."[1] In this soft outcry the entertainer admits to no present pain but confesses to the fear of it.

At the cross, pain is not eliminated, but it is stared down. "God is spirit" (John 4:24), but when he entered the human arena in Christ, he voluntarily opted to have a nervous system. Here at the cross, pain, like a serpent, wraps its coils about the body of our Lord and heralds the ending of his life. I have read the medical reports that tell how Jesus died, so I comprehend the suffering, the suffocation, the screaming lesions in his flesh. But the marvel of it all is that he elected to have the pain. Others may have known equal or greater pain in their passing, but Jesus chose to endure it. In becoming a man, he was made in human likeness, but the glory of this condescension is that he humbled himself and became "obedient unto death, even the death of the cross" (Phil. 2:7–8). It is the "even" in this passage that is the key to his willingness to deal with all that is fully human, including pain.

✛ ✛ ✛

Jesus is no whimpering Savior, complaining of the hurt of it all. He does cry out that he is thirsty (John 19:28), but when they offer him an assuaging narcotic, he would not drink (Mark 15:23). Why? Who can say, except that he was fully locked into our human condition. There would be others, he knew, who would have to taste of pain for which no narcotic would be offered. Jesus wanted to taste of total pain and death as it might be tasted by all humanity.

There can be no greater need than to know that our God is no stranger to pain. He is, as Henri Nouwen pointed out, the wounded healer. To each inquisitor who wants to know where our Messiah can be found, we must say again, "He is outside the city near the gates. He sits bandaged, yet he invites all those who are injured to come to him for healing." He does not heal by waving a magic wand above the hurting. Nor does he traffic in prayer cloths. His healing power derives from his own pain, from having iron spikes driven through his body. With that ugly triumph he can heal.

✛   ✛   ✛

Does this healer ever fail? No. He never fails. He always deals with our pain in complete success. Is this boast too daring? It is neither daring nor is it a boast. Jesus triumphs over our screaming agony by having triumphed over his own crucified nervous system. When he closed his eyes in death at Calvary, after crying "It is finished!" he knew the cooling release from all suffering. Christ deals with *all* pain, either by freeing us from it in this life or kissing us into victorious eternity, where dying itself heals all pain with an everlasting "balm of Gilead" (Jer. 8:22). I have seen Michelangelo's *Pietà* a few times and am always overcome by the tenderness of the mother, holding at last her Son, now set free of all suffering. But it is El Greco's *La Trinidad* that most touches me. In this great painting, the Father is holding the crucified Son, while the Holy Spirit flutters overhead. El Greco captures Christ in the exquisite moment of his final release from pain. He has died—but he is held by his Father. And with

159

the suffering of Immanuel ("God with us"), the pain of all human experience is past.

But let us not characterize all the pain of the cross as only physical. Who can say if the ropes and thorns hurt more than the psychological and spiritual abandonment by those who deserted Jesus in his hour of need? Surely this pain also counts as agony. There are many kinds of pain confronted and beaten by the sovereign and unswerving purpose of Jesus Christ, he who thus becomes the author and finisher of our faith (Heb. 12:2). Jesus perfected, yes, even nullified, the final effects of pain. Cancer might kill the body, but eternity stretching ahead by millennia would find the essence of that person delivered from any lasting effects of pain. This is the outcome of the cross.

The *Via Dolorosa* was not just for Jesus. Oh, it was difficult for him to carry the cross, to stumble under it, to feel the splintered killer crushing him between its own crude weight and the cutting stones of the street. Each time he fell beneath it, he must have remembered again that there was no way out and no turning back. The cross was a killer! To the eyes of the onlookers it seemed clear that it would win and he would lose. The *Via Dolorosa* was a one-way lane that led to death. There was no possible escape.

✠ ✠ ✠

I remember a sister in Christ to whom I once ministered. Her cross was cancer. Her *Via Dolorosa* was a one-way trip through oxygen masks, rubber drainage hoses, and blinking machinery—a kaleidoscope of suffering. She bore the indignity of bedpans and the cruel necessity of having some of her Christian sisters (who served round the clock as volunteer nurses) clean her body and spoon-feed her nourishment. "Every day," she wept, "I ask the

160

Lord to deliver me from this suffering and make me just a little stronger. But no matter how hard I pray, I simply become weaker each day."

I prayed for her, of course, but I understood that the *Via Dolorosa* of any life runs in one direction only. We must travel that road until the cross we are asked to carry has done its final work. Sometimes the pain will stop only when life stops. But it does stop when we enter the presence of Christ. Let us remind ourselves of something pointed out in a previous chapter: the word *finisher,* or *perfecter* in Hebrews 12:2 is the Greek *archegos,* which literally means pioneer or first-goer. Not only did Christ die for us, he was the first-goer into the destructive and threatening world of pain.

✠   ✠   ✠

Indeed, his work on the cross called together the community of the kingdom (see chapter 4). We were mortared into oneness by his dying, but our community reaches its zenith of love when pain enters the picture. When pain strikes a brother or sister, we react instantly with compassion. We join our prayers and hearts and tears so that the one who is hurt can feel our common support. The cross becomes the focal point of our compassion. Through the Savior's pain, we learn about the fellowship of our suffering (Phil. 3:10), and we can look at our suffering comrades and say again with Paul, "We weep with those who weep" (Rom. 12:15). He is describing the caring community when he says, "If one part suffers, every part suffers with it . . ." (1 Cor. 12:26 NIV). We, the community of the cross, shoulder each other's pain and diffuse its great weight. The cross demands nothing less!

Furthermore, we understand that Christ is there to develop within us a more in-depth humanity. Joyce Lan-

161

dorf writes that when she once heard someone brag, "I've never been sick a day in my life," she couldn't help but feel a bit sorry for that person. As she puts it, "Pain and illness produce a quality of aliveness within our souls like nothing else can do."[2] I suspect, too, that it is not possible to be fully human without knowing the suffering caused by human malice or insensitivity. Perhaps this is the reason for the incarnation in general and the crucifixion in particular.

✠ ✠ ✠

There is perhaps one final glory that comes down to us from Calvary. Come with me in a momentary conjecture and see the Christ of the resurrection. Visualize him sharing that terrific breakfast on the shore of Galilee with his disciples (John 21:1–14). They eat together in the wonderful dawn of softly lit sunrise. On the Master's hands as he breaks the bread for them are the stigmata of his recent ordeal. One wonders if, just for a moment, the now-alive Jesus doesn't laugh with his companions as they savor together a newer freedom than they had known before the cross. Jesus' pain and dying was all past. I hope you will not think me fanciful for believing that the resurrected Christ felt that freedom and expressed it with a laughter that he may well have taught to his followers. Why would I say this? Because overcoming past pain always causes us to treasure the present joy.

One young Jew, who knew the terror of a concentration camp, took the trouble to write these words:

> From tomorrow on
> I shall be sad
> From tomorrow on—
> not today.

162

Today I will be glad,
   and every day
      no matter how bitter it may be
   I shall say
From tomorrow on I shall be sad
   not today.[3]

What shall we surmise? Can these words be authentic when spoken by someone who has known a cross? Of course, for following the cross means that the joy of every moment is to be savored. It is the gift of the cross to teach us to know the full flavor of every joy we encounter today.

Let us look for a moment at the entire spectrum of Jesus' life, and at every conceivable pain he endured. It began, no doubt, even as he was being born in human form. The infant Jesus struggled through the birth canal of Mary, sensing her own riveting pain, until he emerged into the life that all humans know. From that moment of infant pain, he began to move toward the cross, where the greatest lessons of pain would be his—and ours.

Between Jesus' makeshift cradle and his empty tomb came his cross. How filled with meaning is the manger where God thrust himself into humanity! More meaningful still is the empty grave, thrown open for an unbelieving world. It was from a shepherd's cave in Judea that Isaiah's word *Immanuel* was first whispered while a maid from Galilee cuddled her infant son to her heart. Yes, the word *Immanuel*— "God with us"—was heard in the stable, but it was not there that the word attained its greatest meaning. Neither the manger nor the mausoleum would say "God with us" as convincingly as the cross.

What a thrilling word is *"Immanuel."* It refers to the life of Jesus Christ, and it says that God is in it with us! This is wonderful news! Here is the excitement of God's stepping out of his immaculate infinity into an impure humanity. When God wished to tell the world, "I am in it with you," he chose an infant's cradle. But when God wished to tell the world, "I am in it with you, *regardless,*" he chose the cross. This is what St. Alphonsus Maria de Liguori meant when he wrote:

> But the Son of God, seeing man thus lost and wishing to save him from death, offered to take upon himself our human nature and to suffer death himself, condemned as a criminal on a cross. "But, my Son," we may imagine the eternal Father saying to him, "think of what a life of humiliations and sufferings Thou wilt have to lead on earth. Thou wilt have to be born in a cold stable and laid in a manger, the feeding trough of beasts. While still an infant, thou wilt have to flee into Egypt, to escape the hands of Herod. After thy return from Egypt, thou wilt have to live and work in a shop as a lowly servant, poor and despised. And finally, worn out with sufferings, thou wilt have to give up thy life on a cross, put to shame and abandoned by everyone." "Father," replied the Son, "all this matters not. I will gladly bear it all, if only I can save man."[4]

✠   ✠   ✠

The energy of the gospel is that "God is in it with us." Without this, Christianity would be like any other religion. The gods served by all other world religions have preserved for themselves the comfort of uninvolvement. These gods generally claim to love humanity, but it is a kind of long-distance love. They hurl parables, challenges, and threats from the heights where they dwell; occasionally they even cast out lightning bolts, visions, tricks, and miracles. But the human predicament has not seriously affected these gods to the extent that they wish to get themselves personally involved. So live the gods of a half-dozen faiths, comfortable in their heavens, kept safe by their starry distance from a suffering, needy world. Meanwhile, their poor underling subjects struggle in troubled existence, crying, praying, and weeping for their attention.

Even the one true God, the Father of our Lord, *before* he sent his Son to the world, usually acted from a rather safe distance. God loved all his subjects, to be sure, particularly those who were downtrodden. He performed a series of miracles to release the Hebrew slaves who had been stamping straw into mud for four hundred years. He split the sea, made manna, brought water from a fissure in a wall of rock, and delivered his laws to Moses. Still, he never came to earth in person. God wanted people to know him in the ages preceding Christ, but he disclosed himself only in a general way: in burning bushes, budding almond rods, and the like.

✠ ✠ ✠

But God got specific at Bethlehem. He left that nebulous, never-never land of heaven and came to a planet that must have seemed a pigsty by comparison. Then, for thirty-three years, men had a miraculous privilege: positive, tangible proof that "God is in it with us." There he was—Creator of the cosmos—jostled among camel drivers, questioned by scholars, laughing, weeping, even asking God for answers, and ultimately dying.

Jesus the Son became the involved God! He probed our human milieu with his manhood. In this total involvement, God shed tears so that our grieving would never again need to occur alone. He knew our heartache and pain by experience. On the cross, God taught us something his previously aloof immortality had obscured: We neither live nor die alone. How misty and ambiguous are all the other gods, flaunting their "foreverness" to the grieving but knowing nothing about human pain. Not *our* God! He learned about pain by suffering. And he learned about death by dying. There was no other way he could say, "I am in all of it, even death, with you."

Shusaku Endo, that noble Japanese Christian statesman, believed that Jesus never made much of an impact on the Japanese people. Because they had heard about mainly the beauty and majesty of Jesus' life, they never understood the crucified Christ, the Jesus who made himself powerless for our salvation. I fear that this sacrificial Christ is the Christ we, too, tend to avoid, for just a glimpse of the dying Savior places great demands on us. God spoke through Isaiah to describe the Suffering Servant and leave no doubt of the legitimacy of those loud demands:

> . . . . he hath no form nor comeliness; and when we shall see him, there is no beauty that we should desire him. He is despised and rejected of men; a man of sorrows, and acquainted with grief; and we hid as it were our faces from him; he was despised, and we esteemed him not. Surely he hath borne our griefs, and carried our sorrows; yet we did esteem him stricken, smitten of God, and afflicted. But he was wounded for our transgressions, he was bruised for our iniquities; the chastisement of our peace was upon him; and with his stripes we are healed (Isa. 53:2b–5 KJV).

Our healing lies in *his* stripes, *his* wounds. Because he hurts, our pain is dealt with. If you understand Jesus' pain, you also know what he meant when he said to take up your cross *daily* (Luke 9:23). None of us knows the exact nature of the cost, but we are not to expect a life free of the probability of crucifixion pain—whether physical, social, or mental. To be involved with the cross is to learn all kinds of pain yet know also that all kinds are healed.

✠   ✠   ✠

The cross, then, becomes the glorious expression of God's total involvement in our world of suffering. Carlyle once protested that Emerson lived a sheltered and peaceable life and never let anything unpleasant into his scheme for living. According to Carlyle, Emerson wanted no worrisome pebbles making ripples in his placid pool of existence. Emerson seemed to Carlyle to be an unrealistic person so uninvolved with trouble that he could not be taken seriously when he gave advice to the troubled. He was like a complacent lifeguard who always keeps himself dry while throwing friendly chitchat to a swimmer who is battling for life itself in an insurgent sea of troubles.

This very accusation might someday have been laid at the feet of the God of Judaism if he had chosen some other way to redeem us, rather than the incarnation and the cross. The cross redeemed us only because it took into account our plight. The wicked deserve damnation, but the spark in humanity that reflects God's image deserves redemption. God got involved because he loved us and knew that his sinful children were suffering.

In one sense God had a dilemma, a conflict between mercy and justice. Despite his warnings, we had disobeyed and should be held accountable. But God also realized that we were trapped by our sin and could not let go of it. Sin is like a sticky piece of candy that a child pulls from the right hand only to find it stuck to the left. To free us, it was not enough for God to know our predicament. He must not only see it; he must feel it. To feel it, he must have flesh that could know the stab of pain and the erosion of disease—flesh that could be crucified. So God became flesh and came to know human existence firsthand. Finally, having experienced even death, he was prepared to offer us life. Surely if God could have thought of some tidier, less expensive way to give us life, he would have done so. But the only way to help us was to get in the world with us.

✠ ✠ ✠

A more ordinary illustration may convey the urgency of our need and the nature of God's response. Suppose a father has taken his family on a picnic at the seaside. It is the most fun they have had together in a good while. The charcoal is gleaming crimson in the brazier. The steaks lie crowded together on aluminum foil. The family can hardly wait until this out-of-doors banquet is a little further underway.

Suddenly the father looks around and sees that his child is missing. His first impulse is to look toward the sea. Instinctively he hurries toward the rushing waters. Ordinarily, he loves the sea's beauty, but now he is filled with dread by the very thought of its power. As he quickens his pace he remembers telling the child to stay close by, but he blames himself for giving all his attention to secondary concerns. He rushes to the shoreline, where he searches for footprints in the sand. Then he sees his child, already swept too far out by the tide to be talked back to safety. If that dearest part of the father is to be rescued, he must dive into the cruel waves himself.

This was precisely God's dilemma. He could no longer call out to us from the safety of eternity's shoreline. Our predicament was too serious for that. If we were to be delivered, God had to throw aside his dignity and aloofness and get into the unpredictable surf of sin and human suffering. The cross came about because of God's wonderful willingness to get involved. As Helmut Thielicke wrote:

> Jesus Christ did not remain at base headquarters in heaven, receiving reports of the world's suffering from below and shouting a few encouraging words to us from a safe distance. No, he left the headquarters and came down to us in the frontline trenches, right down to where we live and worry about what the Bolsheviks may do, where we contend with our anxieties and the feeling of emptiness and futility, where we sin and suffer guilt, and where we must finally die. There is nothing that he did not endure with us. He understands everything.[5]

✠   ✠   ✠

In another of his books, Dr. Thielicke says that it is impossible to learn war in a theater. It occurred to me, after reading this statement, that this is the only kind of war I have ever known. Having been born at a particularly blessed time that made me too young to be involved in one war and too old for the next, I have never served my country in uniform. The only war I have ever known I have seen in theaters or on television. I have only vicariously experienced the incandescence of bursting shells and heard the ear-shattering thunder of explosives. No one would say that I know what war is like. The closest I can come to knowing war firsthand is to visit a veterans' hospital. For me there was really never any war, yet for these the war goes on. The old battlefield lives. The pain continues. They have seen the Pale Horse of Death and know the hell that

169

rides with him. I am but an armchair soldier and hence no soldier at all.

But the cross is there to say that God was no mere spectator in our war against emptiness and death. In Christ, God did not merely observe our coming death. He suffered it ahead of time to prove to us that death's flip side was in reality life eternal. He entered the fray! He is with us!

✠ ✠ ✠

By the time that Jesus had experienced all of his life until Maundy Thursday, he was so much "in it" with us that he refused to get out. He could have left Jerusalem at Passover time. For that matter, he could have avoided going there. He could have left the garden before his arrest. He was not captured by surprise in Gethsemane; he had plenty of opportunity for escape. Even after he had been taken into custody, he was still not in any real danger, for of his own admission he was the Supreme Commander of an immense infantry of angels, who would have delivered him from the cross (Matt. 26:53). But he seemed eager to die.

I doubt that Jesus *wanted* to die, but I do believe that from the very beginning of his earthly ministry he understood its necessity. That necessity was what led him to say, "Except a corn of wheat fall into the ground and die, it abideth alone: but if it die, it bringeth forth much fruit" (John 12:24 KJV). This necessity also entailed the unavoidability of pain.

Nevertheless, we must not see Jesus as the victim of a masochistic martyr complex. He was only thirty-three, an age at which no healthy man in ordinary circumstances would wish himself dead, particularly not Jesus! One sees him as a robust man totally in love with life. He loved to scoop his arms full of children to learn from them their simple wisdom. Yet he was also the sort of man who could never take for granted the splendor of a Galilean sunset as it ignited the broad skies with celestial fire and then settled on the misty, beige waters of Tiberias. This man Jesus found a harmony in everything that his Father touched, and he knew of nothing that the Father had not touched.

No, three decades of life did not find Jesus ready to die. There were so many sermons he had not preached. There was so much misery and hunger he had not had the opportunity to deal with. He longed for a thousand more quiet chats with his friends in Bethany. He loved good food and good conversation. He enjoyed the out-of-doors living he shared with his twelve friends. All of this would be broken off by the cross.

It was there at the cross, however, that a greater issue—our salvation—took the reins of his being. He packed away in self-denial all those wonderful things he so loved. Then courageously he asked God, "Father, what wilt thou?" God answered the question with a squadron of soldiers dispatched for his arrest.

Those few hours following God's answer were to speak with pointed syllables the word *Immanuel*—"God is with us." What a depth of meaning that word took unto itself at the cross! "God is with us" when we experience injustice. "God is with us" when well-meaning friends desert us and our mutual convictions for some more comfortable stand. "God is with us" when our purity and integrity are challenged by circumstances. "God is with us" when we become the object of expensive sport by human sadists. "God is with us" in suffering and when we probe for acceptable answers to ugly questions. Immanuel is here today!

171

This is the real majesty of it; he is our contemporary. Just think of that! We can say *"Immanuel"* with as much meaning as the centurion who ordered the cross to be lifted up against a turbulent sky seething with God's indignation. Keep this straight. *Immanuel* does not mean "God *was* with us." It means "God *is* with us."

William Blake said on his deathbed, "My death songs are not mine."[6] I don't know all he meant by this, but I can guess that his best lessons in joy and pain and human finality had come from a better composer and performer than himself. Jesus the Immanuel God had taught the world the cross song. Christ was with William Blake in his pain; the cross was the symbol of God's continuing presence even in dying.

I had a boyhood chum who never in the early years of our friendship was open to the issue of surrender to Christ. After adolescence we were separated for forty years. At last his company moved him to the city where I had become a pastor. Our friendship was reestablished. At our first meeting he informed me he was carrying a terrible judgment; he was soon to die of cancer.

In the months that he had left to live, my friend embraced Christ as his Savior. Pain was his constant companion, but so was Christ. Somehow the glory of the Christian faith became our absorbing interest. We spoke in his final weeks almost entirely of Christ, that in heaven there would be no death, no crying, no pain (Rev. 21:4). It was as if the ever-present Christ, by promise of a painless eternity, was healing my friend of pain through the glorious power of the surrendering moment. As God had come so long ago to be the Incarnate Christ, my beloved friend became the personification of Christ, teaching all he met the "Immanuel victory" over death and dying.

172

The cross could not blot the word *Immanuel* from the lexicon of belief. Although pain is present in this world, God is still with us. The cross was the end of nothing except Jesus' first coming and the painful condemnation imposed on us by sin. To the contrary, the cross was the *beginning* of everything tinged with meaning. God has been with us in an ever more intimate way since the Roman spear clinched with finality the events of the first Good Friday.

‡   ‡   ‡

How in truth may we say *"Immanuel"* when the historical Jesus is separated from us by the broad gulf of two hundred decades? Is it not fantasy to say that he is yet alive and yet with us? The full import of this issue belongs to the last chapter of this book, but let us say by way of an emphatic preface to that chapter, "Jesus is a living Lord." He is contemporary not just with us but with every generation between his cross and his coming again. To each of the past nineteen centuries he has said *"Immanuel"* and meant it.

So real is Christ's cross in our age that every day some new believer embraces belief in its redemptive work. It continues to stir richer dedication for those wholly owned of Christ Immanuel. God is in this life with us. Jesus, our contemporary Savior, walks our malls, rides our freeways, flies our airlines with us. He will never leave us nor forsake us (Heb. 13:5). He is with us in the shadowy corridors of hospitals, in our fiery instant suffering, and wherever else there is pain. So long as there is pain, the Comforter walks beside us. He is as at home in the Information Age as he was in the first century. He is ours, now and forever. Immanuel! Yesterday! Today! Tomorrow!

173

*Because upon
the first glad Easter day,*

*The stone that sealed
his tomb
was rolled away,*

*So through the
deepening shadows
of death's night,*

*Men see an open door . . .
beyond it, light!*

Ida Norton Munson
Easter Light

10

The Triumph of Transcendence

Living Here, Living Somewhere Else, But Ever Living

e said to them, "It is not for you to know the times or dates the Father has set by his own authority. But you will receive power when the Holy Spirit comes on you; and you will be my witnesses . . . to the ends of the earth."

After he said this, he was taken up before their very eyes, and a cloud hid him from their sight.

They were looking intently up into the sky as he was going, when suddenly two men dressed in white stood beside them. "Men of Galilee," they said, "why do you stand here looking into the sky? This same Jesus, who has been taken *from you into heaven, will come back in the same way you have seen him go into heaven" (Acts 1:7–11 NIV).*

What should be the final lines in the saga of Golgotha? Is there an ending at all? It is incorrect to say that the story was over when the whispers of Christ's breath faded into stillness beneath the mocking letters I.N.R.I.: *Jesus of Nazareth, the King of the Jews.* If his splendid life ended there, the rest of the tale is a powerless piece of human fiction. Two of his influential friends, Nicodemus and Joseph of Arimathea, came to unfasten the Master from the wood, wrap him in a shroud, and entomb him. It is touching to realize that two of his wealthy companions cared this much for him. As touching as it is, however, one still must ask, "Where is the depth of meaning in this tragic event?" Calvary must either end with something more dramatic than the sentimental burial of a kindly carpenter, or we must be willing to replace it with something that offers continuity and significance.

⊹ ⊹ ⊹

It is not the death on the cross but the outcome of that event that offers the greatest meaning for all mankind. The cross remains a powerful symbol because it is the image of the cost of our redemption and Jesus' willingness to pay that price. But the real glory of Christianity is its abstraction—LIFE. It is shallow to oversimplify by saying that the cross symbolizes only death and the resurrection symbolizes life. The cross is an object, a concrete, cold symbol that stands for what we all understand: Jesus' death and ours, too. But the resurrection is a powerful and wonderful truth that cannot be symbolized; while incontrovertibly true, it is too abstract a concept to be captured in a single image.

But the cross does speak to the greatest truth of our faith: *transcendence.* Let us not be afraid of this word. It simply means that the most valuable parts of all we believe are not as concrete as the cross. It is no trick to believe that Jesus died. The cross says that he died and reminds us that so will we. But what is most magnificent cannot be objectified or proven "scientifically." Jesus is alive. Notice I did not say *was* alive, but *is* alive. The resurrection introduces us to a whole battery of truth that we cannot prove. Jesus is alive, but it remains unthinkable to many that this once-dead man, who had walked on earth in the era of the Caesars, stepped out of his tomb and is even now as much alive as he ever was before he was carried into it.

Transcendent truths are like that. They are hard to believe because they exceed the limits of human experience and penetrate beyond all logical categories of possibility. The truth of the risen Lord was doubted by the apostles themselves when they first encountered it (Luke 24:11). After the disciples were changed by this overwhelming transcendent truth and could admit that while dead men generally don't live again, their Master did, they went out to preach the resurrection. The good news didn't go over too well with some people they tried to convince. They told the Sanhedrin (Acts 4:10), but these priests and elders didn't believe. They told the Sanhedrin a second time (Acts 5:30–32), but they still didn't believe. When Stephen told them again, they were enraged and stoned him to death (Acts 7). Paul finally accepted the truth, but only after he was knocked off his beast on the way to Damascus (Acts 9:1–19). But only a few believed Paul when he preached in Athens (Acts 17:16–34). In Caesarea, King Agrippa was not convinced. When Festus, governor of Judea, heard Paul's testimony, he stood and shouted, "You are out of your mind, Paul! Your great learning is driving you insane" (Acts 26:24 NIV).

Christians view Calvary as a historical truth. But the resurrection is a transcendent truth. Both of them are equally true, but the latter concept is a bit harder for some to believe. Still, Christianity is founded on this transcendent truth. No one doubts that men die, even on crosses to which they willingly yield. Harder to believe is that once dead they continue living. Yet this is the greatest truth and the imperative that creates the Christian faith. The Greek word *anastasis* means "to stand again." And so he did! And when our Savior stood that first Easter, he stood not only so we would notice *he* was no longer dead, but also to take a stand for the transcendent truth of the resurrected life. Christianity cannot survive without this truth. In his poem "Seven Stanzas at Easter," John Updike wrote:

Make no mistake: if He rose at all
it was as His body;
if the cells' dissolution did not reverse, the molecules
reknit, the amino acids rekindle,
the Church will fall.

Let us not mock God with metaphor,
Analogy, sidestepping transcendence;
making of the event a parable, a sign painted in the
faded credulity of earlier ages:
let us walk through the door.

178

Let us not seek to make it less monstrous,
for our own convenience, our own sense of beauty,
lest, awakened in one unthinkable hour, we are
    embarrassed by the miracle,
and crushed by remonstrance.[1]

Updike warned us that although the resurrection is transcendent and unfathomable, if we try to sidestep this truth, the church will fall.

It is my judgment that for all its apparent successes the Christian church at the end of the twentieth century is in grave danger (no pun intended) of not merely "sidestepping transcendence" but of abandoning it altogether. What has brought about this deplorable state? Who can say? Perhaps we have grown too matter-of-factly scientific about our bodies. I see nothing unspiritual about donating our bodies to science and our organs to help others live. And living wills are a smart way to be judicious in the stewardship of all we are physiologically. But is it possible that in frankly discussing the economical use of our bodies we have begun to assume that we are *only* biology; a physiological system of interchangeable tissues and organs?

Further, the more we live in our stainless-steel and computerized technocracy, the less we hear our preachers talking about heaven and hell and eternity. Although Jesus is fervently preached by most twentieth-century preachers, he is mostly a Jesus of the moment. The Jesus of the evangelical community is rapidly in danger of becoming the Christ who handles current stress, or makes us popular as politicians or show-biz converts. In past generations the churches were absorbed in preaching "pie in the sky by and by," but now we are hearing less and less of sky

ONCE UPON A TREE

pie and more and more of "the good life" being here and now.

The church's ultimate question once was *ultimate!* It dealt with eternity. Our hymns were about "The Sweet By and By," "Beulah Land," and "Zion," to which we were marching. And Zion was a land as real as Chicago in the rural church in which I found Christ. Today Chicago is the more real. We don't use the word *saved* in any ultimate sense. We have been saved, but we will not be saved in any real sense once this life is over. Hell, once a never-ending category, is now only bad conditioning or ghetto sociology. Psychologists have brought a new counsel to God's people, and while their counsel is helpful in the all-important world of relationships, it comes often with little sense of the importance of the world that's on the way.

The depravity of our sermons is that they have forgotten to mention that there is a new world on the way. We speak of Jesus only in terms of his power over our current misery. We almost never mention that he is also the Christ of the New Jerusalem that one day in the future (we so rarely mention) will descend from God out of heaven.

Recently I preached a sermon to a large gathering of evangelicals in which I referred to hell, the destiny of those who die outside of Christ. While the reference was made in passing, I was told afterward that the reference "marred" my presentation. We have arrived at a here-and-now theology, it seems, in which every transcendent category is lost.

╬   ╬   ╬

A friend of mine told me about being shown through a pre-Revolutionary War cemetery in Charleston, South

Carolina. The guide was pointing out the various tomb-stones and commenting on those who were buried there. The history buffs in the group were fascinated by the tombstones of these founders of the American dream. Noticing that so many of the two- and three-hundred-year-old stones had weather-eroded inscriptions like "entered Immortality, July 3, 1756" or "Gone to God, May 3, 1734," the guide said, "You will observe that many of the remarks are about the afterlife, but we all know how we feel about this!" Then the guide winked at the battery of tourists who were furiously scratching his remarks onto their note sheets. My friend said it was the wink that so unnerved him. For that wink signified the tragic loss of transcendent truth in our day.

✠ ✠ ✠

Jesus' victory over death is inseparable from his teachings about eternity. There is little use in preaching that Jesus came back from the dead if there was nowhere for him to go. He taught us that there are afterlife categories: heaven and hell. And these ideas are as true and transcendent as his own emergence from the tomb. Let us not become the captives of "this world" religion. Let us not make of the risen Christ, who walks the technological world, a homeless Messiah who has lost his transcendence, a vagrant with no eternity to preside over.

In a sense, the church growth movement has contributed to this loss of transcendence. It has majored on the gospel that twentieth-century people want to hear, rather than the one they need to hear. Many of the megachurch pastors speak with pride of building multi-thousand member churches with a gospel that is "user-friendly." To start these churches, they often, of their own admission, asked their community constituency what kind of church and sermons it would take to get people to go to church. Once the community had told the church what it must be to get their support, the church became all its constituents demanded. While it is difficult to imagine Jeremiah or Jesus starting a church in this way, the populist definition in many cases has become the norm in the megachurch. When the world writes the definition of the church, we may be sure all transcendent categories will be missing. Most community residents (and the all-important baby boomers, especially) are not enthusiastic about sermons on heaven, hell, and the crucified life. They prefer something which will gently massage their narcissism with "how-to" and "fix-it" sermons. Thus transcendence at first took a back seat to sermons on stress, relationships, and leisure-entertainment homilies. As the transcendent was increasingly ignored, the heavenless, hell-less, resurrectionless gospel was glitzed with humor and bright lights and lost the important aspects of its transcendent cause.

✠   ✠   ✠

In the cross itself are hidden four of Christ's "last words," which testify to his transcendence and to the reality of eternity. If we look at them one by one, we shall see that the cross and the resurrection are one. For in God every truth is transcendent. It is not as though the cross as an event is the prisoner of time and her sister, the resurrection, is liberated from harsh history. No, they are both part of the great transcendent incarnation. The Jesus who died was not of this earth (John 6:38; 18:36). Through his coming he made of his whole life here an issue of transcendence wherein the realm of time is invaded by the eternal. On the cross he makes that clear.

"My God, why . . .?" (Matt. 27:46) is a cry from the cross reminding us even as he dies that while he doesn't understand in his human form the pain his Father asks him to bear, he is still talking to his Father. This bit of conversation, along with his prayer asking God to forgive his executioners (Luke 23:34), proves that Jesus is in conversation with a transcendent realm beyond the here and now world. This conversation is enough to let the cross establish the reality of eternity.

But there are other cross cries—for instance, "Father, into thy hands I commend my Spirit" (Luke 23:46). Again the transcendent world of his Father is a grand reality that issues from the cross.

"It is finished" (John 19:30) is the real signal from the cross that the whole transcendent plan of God is completed. Here it must be that God stamps A on the celestial report card. Jesus is not saying "I am finished," signaling his death. He is saying that the incarnation with its magnificent objectives is done. We are saved; heaven—transcendent heaven—is peopled with all of us who will believe.

⚔ ⚔ ⚔

But the cross cry that most clearly addresses the transcendent world is: "Today you will be with me in paradise" (Luke 23:43). Here from the cross we see the juncture of the present moment and the eternal moment. We are taught the utter truth of two who are dying. Redeemer and renegade, though suffocating and bleeding, look past the pain. And where their bloody faces focus we see the dim outlines of the celestial city. Stephen at his death saw it, too, and looked past the gates of paradise to the very throne room and said in effect, "Kill me if you must, but my death is but a promotion. For I see heaven open and the Son of Man standing on the right hand of God" (Acts 7:56).

From the cross the testimony continues to spill forth. There is a living Christ and there is heaven and the best truths are transcendent. John cried in the Apocalypse, "I was in the Spirit on the Lord's Day . . . and I saw among the lampstands someone like a son of man . . . and his voice was like the sound of rushing waters" (Rev. 1:10, 12–13, 15). Paul spoke of being caught up to the third heaven (2 Cor. 12:2), and Isaiah said, "I saw the LORD seated on a throne, high and exalted . . ." (Isa. 6:1 NIV).

✢   ✢   ✢

How then are we to take in this transcendence? The cross must be our teacher. How will the cross do its work? Well, to begin with, we must not tell the story of Christ as the tale of a well-meaning martyr. To see clearly the outcome of the cross, we first allow the purple shadows of Good Friday to steal hope, purpose, and meaning from everything that Jesus ever claimed. Then we must see the gray dawn of the middle day, when the Son of God, reduced to a human corpse, lay silent in the grave. Here was despair that could find no resolution. To every eye it appeared that he was dead—forever dead! Wrapped in silent parables and soundless songs, he who claimed to be "the life" was dead. The mists of that middle day blurred eyes with grief and gripped the hearts of believers with the painful consciousness that they had given him their allegiance in vain. So the weary weekend was over. And it was just at that place where the long, long, second day faded into the next that God wrote a victorious epilogue to Friday's defeat.

The cross was God's finest effort to demonstrate his love, but we would never have stopped to consider it without the resurrection. And, without the majesty and sacrifice of the cross, we would have forgotten the resurrection in a fortnight. The resurrection is as historical as the cross, and they are *both* imperative to our faith.

The weird hypothesis that Matthew Arnold presented in *Obermann Once More* is untrue:

> Now he is dead! Far hence he lies
> In the lorn Syrian town,
> And on his grave with shining eyes,
> The Syrian stars look down.

To be sure, this is where the cross leaves Jesus; he is alone and dead in a Middle East tomb. Were the cross the end of it all, someone might someday discover Jesus' grave covered by the debris of time. Since that first Easter, however, it will forever be impossible to find a headstone marked "Jesus of Nazareth" with the date of his decease chiseled out in Roman numerals. He is alive! God has raised him from the dead! All men must believe this, for it is the pier on which personal salvation rests. So imperative is the resurrection truth for mankind that none can know salvation without believing it. Wrote Paul: "That if thou shalt confess with thy mouth the Lord Jesus, and shalt believe in thine heart that God hath raised him from the dead, thou shalt be saved" (Rom 10:9 KJV).

As previously mentioned, when Paul made his defense before Agrippa and Festus, he spoke of how he had come to believe in Christ. His testimony was well received until he made mention of the resurrection; then he was accused of madness. When Paul spoke on Mars Hill, the logicians balked at his speaking of the resurrection. Where the cross gives way to the crown, Christianity becomes hard for many to believe. Logicians always balk at a concept that defies "sound reasoning," as the resurrection surely does. But the solid bulwark of Christianity defends its belief in the resurrection of Christ as vigorously as it defends the cross of Christ.

If the resurrection truth seems hard for us, who have the New Testament witness as a backdrop, we can immediately see how hard it must have been for the core of Christ's disciples, who were confronted by it without the advantage of historical perspective. Imagine the women at the tomb as they discover that the dead Jesus is really the living Jesus. Babbling excitedly, they rush to report the news to the apostles. Understandably, the apostles are dumbfounded by the incoherent chatter of these women and are very skeptical of their report.

Then Jesus, every whit alive, walks in on them. They are gripped by the terror that springs from the realm of the supernatural and the occult. Two or three of them probably pinch themselves to be sure they are awake. Others try to talk themselves out of what their eyes tell them is there before them. Surely all of them blink as though the rapid shutting of their eyelids will erase the specter. Suddenly, like a radiant burst of glory, the same truth dawns on them that had come earlier to those excited women. It is true! Jesus is alive!

"And if Christ be not risen, then is our preaching vain, and your faith is also vain" (1 Cor. 15:14 KJV). The *sine qua non* of our faith is the resurrection. This is the outstanding, unique factor of Christianity. We do not embrace the Christian religion because there was a cross, but because the outcome of the cross was the resurrection. If Christ be dead, what real improvement is Christianity over a score of other lofty philosophies? Either Christ has risen from the grave, or we are fools for believing so. Either Christ is alive, or the cross was a black hour, for it was the end of a brilliant little starburst of ethics and positivism. Either the resurrection happened, or the cross must issue this solemn pronouncement: "Alas, he was only a man and we have stolen his life and breath. We are all orphans. God had no son. We have no Father in heaven. I have proven he who made such claims to be a fraud." But this pronouncement is true *only* if the resurrection never happened!

✠   ✠   ✠

Of course, being children whom the modern age has nearly weaned from transcendence, we may find the Lord's return to life "unbelievable." It is beyond our scientific understanding. It is not biological. It is illogical and cannot be proven objectively. It is for these reasons that many have shelved *The Resurrection* in the children's section of fantasies, make-believe, and tales of the Brothers Grimm, where the dead prince is brought back to life and "They all lived happily ever after."

In its earliest discovery by the women, the resurrection is a joyful madness: insanely "unbelievable" because it is so instantaneous, yet overwhelmingly true. According to John's account, after seeing him alive, they ran to bring the report to John and Simon Peter, who rushed to the empty tomb and "believed," when they saw the discarded burial cloths. Soon afterward, Jesus appeared to his disciples, though Thomas was not with them at the time. One can imagine Simon Peter telling Thomas about it later: "Thomas, we have seen the Lord! He's alive!" But Thomas is skeptical about such an impossibility. He sticks his tongue in his cheek and shakes his head "yes" in such a way that you can tell he means "not a chance of it."

Then Thomas says, "Sure, Peter—sure, you did. You saw him." Then he adds explosively, "Who in the world do you think you're trying to outwit? Peter, I watched him die! I saw him like some tortured animal try in vain to cradle his head against the vertical beam of the cross. I watched him till his faithful head slumped forward on his lifeless breast. Then I watched the man with the spear make sure he was dead. It was gruesome, but I was there and I saw it all. He's dead, Peter!"

Then perhaps Thomas would have leveled the same charge of insanity against the report of the apostles as they had earlier laid at the feet of the women. "My dear friends," Thomas might have said, "you have not seen Jesus. At least, you have not seen him alive. You have been in the sun too long without your caps. You saw a man in a seamless robe whose stature was the same perhaps. You saw some bulk in the dark and mistook it for Jesus. Maybe you dreamed he was alive. And Peter, you saw him because you loved him so much that you wanted to see him. I love him, too, but get hold of yourself. Neither of us will ever see him again. He's dead! Dead! Dead!"

Then come more of those "silent" days when Jesus does not show himself to his apostles. Finally, when Thomas is present with the others, the matchless Master of Life breaks in on the reverie of the group. Thomas, his doubts now erased, falls down in submission to the Christ of Kept Promises and says in a voice choked with emotion, "My Lord and my God!" (John 21:28).

╬   ╬   ╬

It was hard for the disciples to accept the resurrection; they were too close to it. It was impossible for them to stand back from a distance of twenty centuries and view it objectively as we do. But accept it they did! In truth, nearly all of them were later martyred, rather than say it did not happen. (One cannot help but wonder if we who have that historical overview would be as unyielding in our defense of the doctrine.) Men will sometimes tell lies, but they will not die for those lies. Each of these men died still clinging to the "unbelievable" transcendent truth that Jesus had risen from the dead.

There are many who say there was no resurrection, but all of the New Testament witnesses believed the resurrection to be a *fact* of history. So have the real defenders of the faith in every generation. As Peter Marshall once said, the resurrection is "historically" true:

> The resurrection of Christ was regarded by the disciples as something which is as indisputable historically as the death of President Wilson. It did not occur to them, as they spoke or as they wrote, to argue about it, any more than it would occur to a senator making a speech to say: "Since the death of President Wilson, *that is to say if he is really dead. . . .*"[2]

✠   ✠   ✠

As surely as Pontius Pilate was a real historical figure, so was Jesus of Nazareth. As surely as the cross really happened, so did the resurrection become its joyous outcome. We who believe must regain the lost imperative of lifting up the resurrection as central to Christian teaching. In contrasting the importance of the cross and the resurrection, we need to remind ourselves that Christ was dead for only three days, but he has now been alive for two thousand years. We need to recall to consciousness that his return from the grave is the all-important victory that has kept Christianity out of the graveyard of other lofty philosophies and religions.

The risen Christ, made alive again by his Father's power, is the only reason we have for remembering the cross. So we must forget the "Messiah of the media," who takes so much film to die and so little to rise again. The resurrection is too important to be shelved as an "incidental" area of Jesus' existence and teaching.

We must also cease this business of talking as though his return to life was only the momentary outcome of the cross. This cannot be accomplished so long as we speak of the resurrection in the past tense, as if it were all over. The resurrection is not a thing of the past and therefore can neither be forgotten nor taken for granted. It is continuous, right down to the present. This very moment Jesus is still living. His life extends across all time from the Caesars to the Space Age. Indeed, his life is the blessed incarnate life of eternity. The resurrection is the recurrent theme in the symphony of the centuries, the golden thread woven into the fabric of time itself.

The resurrection meant triumph to the disillusioned apostles who had given Christ their livelihood, allegiance, and devotion. It is *our* only shot at hope and meaning. Just as the resurrection tied together again the broken cords of existence and swept away the despair of Christ's apostles, let it bind us to something more meaningful than an intellectualized Christ who is but a gilded psychiatrist or pious moralist for the current generation. Sanity itself proceeds from the cross and its glorious outcome. His life is our life, too. We have no life if he does not live.

Through the mist of that long-ago morning moved a cluster of women whose tearstained faces glinted silver with unfulfilled promises. Soon those same women returned to report a phrase that ricocheted in triumph through the lonely canyons of human existence: "He is risen!" has proven that death is only temporary. In Jesus' case it lasted only three days. In our case it may last longer, but now our grave—like his—holds no threat, only possibilities!

The greatest truth, the *truest* truth, is transcendent. We are alive. We will have none wink at us and tell us his resurrection is "sky pie." The earth quaked, the rocks split, and Jesus walked out of the tomb. His very footfalls made hell tremble and shook the cosmos. So, when the unborn sun of any Easter morning shoots its shafts of promise through the east, let us remember that God is ever there to restore our crushed hopes and our lifeless existence. How marvelously God knows how to spell "triumph" for *every* morning.

The writer of the Book of Job sought the answer to his plaguing question, "If a man die, shall he live again?" But we now have the answer! Yes, he *shall* live again! It makes no matter how we die, for even the excruciating and torturous death of the cross was illusory and not binding. The resurrection offers all of us in every generation the same assurance: Jesus is alive. Life without death is possible. Death is not a threat to genuine life. It is but a paper tiger that is no longer free to terrorize us once we know the truth about the outcome of the cross. Death is but a temporary inconvenience that separates our smaller living from our greater being.

The resurrection is the glorious crown of triumph on the exalted head of tragedy. The despair of Good Friday has been superseded by Christ's return to life. The outcome of the cross is that he has overcome death. Because he is alive and will reign forever, we, too, will overcome death.

Hallelujah!

Notes

Chapter 2: *The Wood of the New Agreement*

1. Bruce Cockburn, cited in Gail & Jill Perry, eds., *A Rumor of Angels* (New York: Ballantine Books, 1989), p. 111.

2. Dylan Thomas, "Do Not Go Gentle into That Good Night" (1952).

3. Francis Thompson, "The Hound of Heaven" (1893).

4. Priscilla J. Owens, "Jesus Saves!" *The Hymnal for Worship and Celebration* (Waco, Texas: Word Music, 1986), #306.

5. Fanny J. Crosby, "Near the Cross," *The Hymnal for Worship and Celebration* (Waco, Texas: Word Music, 1986), #385.

Chapter 3: *The Timbers of Grief*

1. Thomas Moore, "Come, Ye Disconsolate," *The Hymnal for Worship and Celebration* (Waco, Texas: Word Music, 1986), #416.

2. Thomas Dooley, *The Night They Burned the Mountain* (as condensed in *Reader's Digest 40th Anniversary Treasury*, The Reader's Digest Association, 1961), pp. 341–342.

3. Thomas à Kempis, *Of the Imitation of Christ*, trans. Abbot Justin McCann (New York: New American Library, 1959), p. 147.

Chapter 4: *The Community of the Cross*

1. Avis B. Christianson, "Blessed Redeemer," *Baptist Hymnal* (Nashville: Convention Press, 1975), #109.

2. Charles Malik, "Trust Your Instincts, Mrs. Jones!" *Guideposts* 16 (May 1961):5–6.

3. Carl J. C. Wolf, *Jonathan Edwards on Evangelism* (Grand Rapids: William B. Eerdmans, 1958), p. ix.

4. William Shakespeare, *Hamlet*.

Chapter 5: *The Tree of Treachery*

1. Catherine Marshall, ed., *Mr. Jones, Meet the Master* (New York: Fleming H. Revell, 1958), p. 145.

Chapter 6: *Who Caused the Cross?*

1. John Bowring, "In the Cross of Christ I Glory," *Baptist Hymnal* (Nashville: Convention Press, 1975), #70.

Chapter 7: *The Death of Death*

1. Musetta Gilman, "Memo to Death," *Trails* (Detroit: Harlo Press, 1986), p. 58.
2. John Chrysostom, *Religious Quotations*
3. Benjamin Franklin, cited in Gail & Jill Perry, eds., *A Rumor of Angels* (New York: Ballantine Books, 1989), p. 151.
4. Edward Chinn, "To Illustrate—Death," *Preaching*, March-April 1991, p. 56.
5. Catherine Marshall, ed., *Mr. Jones, Meet the Master* (New York: Fleming H. Revell, 1958), p. 95.
6. Albert Camus, *The Fall*, trans. Justin O'Brien (New York: Vintage Books, 1956), p. 11.

Chapter 8: *The Dying Life*

1. Cited in Helmut Thielicke, *Christ and the Meaning of Life*, trans. John W. Doberstein (New York: Harper & Row, 1962), p. 15.
2. John White, *The Race* (Downers Grove, Ill.: InterVarsity Press, 1984), p. 141.
3. Cited in Porter Routh, "How Does God Measure?" *Baptist Program*, November 1963, p. 10.
4. St. Theresa, cited in St. Alphonsus Liguori, *Love God and Do What You Please!* trans. C. D. McEnniry, ed. M. J. Huber (Liguori, Mo.: Liguori Publications, 1978), p. 85.
5. Harold Kushner, *When All You've Ever Wanted Isn't Enough* (New York: Pocket Books, 1986), p. 25.
6. G. K. Chesterton, *"St. Francis of Assisi,"* in *Basic Chesterton* (Springfield, Ill.: Templegate Publishers, 1984), p. 26.
7. Ibid., p. 29.

Chapter 9: *The Piercing of Pain*

1. Cited in Arthur C. McGill, *Suffering: A Test of Theological Method*, Paul Ramsey & William F. May, foreword (Philadelphia: The Westminster Press, 1982), p. 41.

2. Joyce Landorf, *Mourning Song* (Old Tappan, N.J.: Fleming H. Revell, 1974), p. 155.

3. Cited in Tim Hansel, *When I Relax I Feel Guilty* (Elgin, Ill.: David C. Cook Publishing, 1979), pp. 61–62.

4. *The Catholic Family Book of Novenas* (New York: John J. Crawley, 1956), p. 2.

5. Helmut Thielicke, *Christ and the Meaning of Life*, trans. John W. Doberstein (New York: Harper & Row, 1962), p. 15.

6. Cited in Malcolm Muggeridge, *A Third Testament* (New York: Ballantine Books, 1988), p. 90.

Chapter 10: *The Triumph of Transcendence*

1. John Updike, "Seven Stanzas at Easter," cited in D. Bruce Lockerbie, *The Liberating Word: Art and the Mystery of the Gospel* (Grand Rapids, Mich.: William B. Eerdmans, 1974), pp. 104–105.

2. Catherine Marshall, ed., *Mr. Jones, Meet the Master* (New York, Fleming H. Revell, 1958), p. 108.